LOCOMOTION PAPERS

The Stoke to Market Drayton Line

and Associated Canals and Mineral Branches

by
C.R. Lester

PIPE GATE STATION

THE OAKWOOD PRESS

© Oakwood Press & C.R. Lester 2001

British Library Cataloguing in Publication Data
A Record for this book is available from the British Library
ISBN 0 85361 293 5

First Printed 1983
Printed by Blenheim Colour Ltd, Oxford.

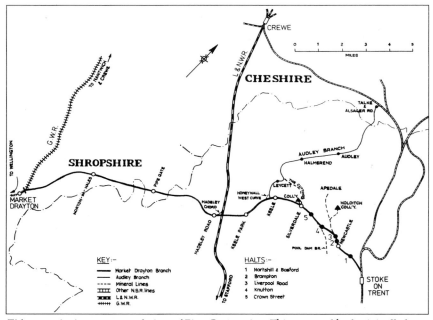

Title page: A picture postcard view of Pipe Gate station. This postcard had originally been posted in Woore in August 1910. *J. Alsop Collection*

Front cover: A view of North Staffordshire Railway 2-4-0T No. 48 in immaculate condition. This locomotive saw many years service on the Stoke to Market Drayton line. *J. Alsop Collection*

Published by The Oakwood Press (Usk), P.O. Box 13, Usk, Mon., NP15 1YS.
E-mail: oakwood-press@dial.pipex.com
Website: www.oakwood-press.dial.pipex.com

CHAPTER 1

THE COMING OF THE CANALS

This short history began as a detailed study of the Stoke-on-Trent to Market Drayton branch railway line and its canal antecedents, but just as one railway leads to another, so research begets research and the end product includes some account of the other 'Drayton' railways, whether constructed or not. Chronologically, however, pride of place belongs to the North Staffordshire Railway Company — or 'Knotty' as it became familiarly known, from the Stafford knot incorporated in its official emblem.

Unlike many of its ambitious contemporaries, the North Stafford-shire was remarkably unassuming in its choice of title, for although its operational and administrative centre was at Stoke-on-Trent, in the very heart of the Potteries, the company's lines extended eventually into parts of Derbyshire, Cheshire and Shropshire. Moreover, if the very considerable running powers exercised over other companies' territories were taken into account, the Knotty's activities could be observed as far afield as Liverpool, Manchester, Wellingborough, Nottingham and along the holiday coast of North Wales; indeed, by the year 1900 the NSR was regularly working upwards of 400 miles of 'foreign' lines — almost twice the length of its own system. Let it be said that these running powers were reciprocal and of such mutual benefit that the absorption of this comparatively small provincial undertaking by one or another of its influential neighbours was firmly resisted and successfully avoided until dissolution into the London Midland & Scottish organisation followed the national grouping of 1923. As E L Ahrons suggested, 'Run over but not crushed' would have been a fitting motto for the North Staffordshire Railway Company.

At the same time, it has to be admitted that the Knotty's excursion into Shropshire amounted only to one branch line, the Shropshire part of which measured little more than six miles. This 'Market Drayton branch' may at first glance be seen as an insignificant cross-country feeder, serving a handful of rather remote intermediate stations and of no particular importance, but the fact that the bulk of its construction was completed so late as 1870 is in no way a true indication of its role in the intrigues of the mid-Victorian railway scene. Some twenty-five years earlier the first section of the branch, from Stoke to Newcastle, had been included in the Knotty's act of incorporation, but its origins were set in pre-railway days. Eighteenth-century England witnessed tremendous advances in methods of inland transport; roads were improved and the turnpike system extended, rivers were made navigable on a considerable scale, the first commercial canals were constructed and the first iron tram-ways were laid down in the vicinity of coal pits and stone quarries. In few areas of the country was there a greater need for improved communications than in North Staffordshire, where the pottery industry — rapidly developing under the leadership of such far-sighted men as Josiah Wedgwood — laboured under considerable difficulties in the conveyance of both raw materials and finished goods. In 1759, when Wedgwood first set up in business at Burslem, all such articles had to be carried by pack horse or waggon to and from the nearest river port, either on the Weaver (at Winsford), the Trent (at Willington, east of Burton upon Trent) or the Severn (at Bridgnorth or Bewdley). The overland distances thus involved ranged between 20 miles (to Winsford) and almost 60 miles (to Bewdley) and the entire process was subject to the seasonal hazards of floods, snow and frost. The high cost of this time-consuming method, together with the ever present risk of breakages and pilfering, prompted Wedgwood and some of his fellow manufacturers to seek a swifter and more profitable way of transporting their wares — which were already in increasing demand in London and on the Continent — and in 1766 parliamentary sanction was obtained for the construction of a waterway to connect the rivers Trent and Mersey, serving the Potteries in its course. This 'Trent & Mersey' or 'Grand Trunk' navigation, which was engineered by James Brindley, threaded its way along the western fringe of the expanding industrial areas of Tunstall, Burslem and Hanley before leaving the Potteries at Stoke, and was opened to traffic throughout its ninety-three miles length in 1777. The ridge of high land linking Harecastle Hill (under which a 2,880 yards long tunnel had to be driven), Porthill, Basford and Harts Hill prevented any direct incursion of Brindley's canal into the ancient borough of Newcastle-under-Lyme and although the town's burgesses petitioned Parliament for a branch canal from Stoke, some twenty years were to elapse before that particular desire was fulfilled.

However, other steps were soon taken to introduce the new means of transport to Newcastle, for in 1775 Sir Nigel Gresley and his son, Nigel Bowyer Gresley, who owned large tracts of coal- and ironstone-bearing land at Apedale, had obtained an Act of Parliament to construct a waterway from their pits to a basin on the northern edge of the borough, a distance of approximately three miles. The promoters undertook to supply coals to the inhabitants of Newcastle at a price of 5s 0d (25p) per ton for a term of twenty-one years (and thereafter 5s 6d to 6s 0d (27½ to 30p) per ton for a similar term) and 'to keep a stock or wharf for the consumption of the town under a penalty of £40.' This wharf lay immediately south-west of the latter-day Liverpool Road railway bridge and halt and was cut off from the rest of 'Gresley's canal' in 1850-1 by the extension of the future Market Drayton branch railway from Newcastle to Knutton Junction, but a coal wharf remained on the site until the late 1930s and provided 'best steam coals' to a diminishing number of traction engines on their ponderous journeys up and down the main road to the North West. Identifiable traces of the canal have disappeared in quite recent years, chiefly since the development of the Loomer and Holditch industrial estates at Chesterton, although Brymbo Road — leading to the Brymbo (alias Holditch) colliery — was laid along the former canal embankment in 1938. The Apedale valley itself has undergone drastic changes since World War II and today, near the site of the old Burley colliery, one capstone of an erstwhile bridge over the canal is only just discernible at the new ground level.

The mining industry generally was now beginning to benefit from the introduction of machinery, and improved methods of drainage enabled working to be carried out at much lower levels than had been possible hitherto. The coal seams in this corner of north-west Staffordshire were reputed to be among the richest in the country and in their heyday they supported a wide spread of collieries and small mines ranging from Talke to Madeley. The six-inch maps of the district are liberally sprinkled with old shafts, and despite large-scale opencast mining operations in recent times, vast reserves remain. The fortunate combination of abundant coal deposits with overlying iron-bearing clays was not unknown to earlier inhabitants of these parts and there is archaeological evidence that coal and iron were utilised hereabouts by the occupying Roman power in about the second century A.D. Furnaces were certainly established at both Apedale and Knutton Heath (Silverdale) by the mid-seventeenth century and Dr Plot, writing in 1685, extolled the virtues of Apedale coal and ironstone which were then being worked by Sir John Bowyer. By the late eighteenth century the principal landowners were John Crewe Offley (created first Lord Crewe in 1806), Ralph Sneyd (1723-93) and the Bowyer Gresleys of Apedale. The Sneyd family had lived in the area since the beginning of the fifteenth century and in 1544 Sir William Sneyd acquired the manor of Keele, where the first Hall was built in 1581. The Gresleys were later to be joined in marriage to the Heathcotes (of Audley and Manchester) and these four families held an effective monopoly of the immense mineral wealth of the district. Nevertheless, better transport facilities were essential to the proper exploitation of these natural resources and Gresley's canal had provided a tentative step in that direction, but by the closing years of the century the Industrial Revolution had produced new and urgent pressures and the time was ripe for expansion. The replacement of charcoal by coal and coke was by then complete and the first coke-fired furnace had been in use at Apedale since 1770. From 1783 the Apedale works were rented by the South Staffordshire firm of Parker, of Tipton, and some eight years later Walter Sneyd (1752-1829) opened his first ironworks at Silverdale, or Knutton Heath as it was then known. The advantages of a national system of navigable waterways were becoming increasingly recognised and in the 1790s three separate schemes were launched in attempts to rectify the local situation. The most ambitious of these was the projected Commercial Canal of 1796, of which Sir Nigel Bowyer Gresley was one of the chief promoters and which aimed to connect the Chester Canal at Nantwich with the Apedale terminus of the Gresley canal. Having reached Newcastle the route lay via Cheadle and Uttoxeter to join the existing canal at Ashby-de-la-Zouche and the completed system would have formed a continuous line of communication between London and the River Dee. The scheme was opposed by the Trent & Mersey, whose waters were to have been used near Burton and other rival factions brought about the collapse of the project in 1797.

A second scheme was more fruitful for in 1795 an independent company obtained an Act of Parliament (not without some opposition from Sir Nigel Bowyer Gresley) to construct a canal from the T & M at Stoke over level ground to a basin just south of Brook Lane at Newcastle, an overall distance of four miles. The canal would pass 'through the village (sic) of Stoke, between the works of Thomas Wolfe and Josiah Spode' a stipulation being that no water was to be taken from the River Trent 'except at times of flood . . . nor from the spring in the village which supplies the engine of Thomas Wolfe . . .' The works were completed in about 1800 but the Brook Lane basin formed the nearest practicable point to the Liverpool Road terminus of Gresley's canal, which lay uphill across the busy town centre and there remained the problem of devising a means of joining the two 'navigations'. The solution was seen as a combination of canal and railway, and in 1798 Sir N B Gresley, Robert Edensor Heathcote and John Wedgwood were primarily responsible for promoting the New-castle-under-Lyme Junction Canal. Even so, a difference in levels of over 60 feet had still to be overcome and the enabling Act of Parlia-ment included provision for the 'making and maintaining (of) a navigable canal, or canal and inclined plane or railway, from and out of the Newcastle-under-Lyme Canal to the Canal of Sir Nigel Bowyer Gresley'. The same Act sanctioned the building of railways to connect Leycett, Silverdale and the Brook Lane basin, none of which was constructed, and the canal in its final form ran for 1⅛ miles over level ground to a terminus in what are today the public gardens known as Stubbs Walks, then a part of the Stubbs Field.

Branching eastwards from Gresley's canal just north of the contem-porary cotton mill (about 500 yards short of the Liverpool Road basin) the Junction Canal passed almost at once under the turnpike road and

NEWCASTLE CANALS AND ASSOCIATED RAILWAYS.

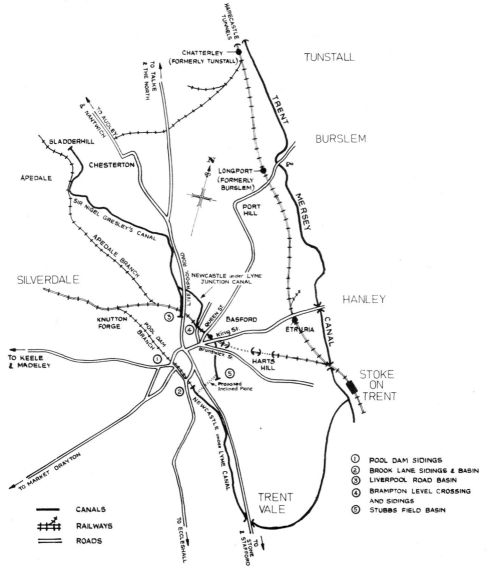

TUNSTALL

BURSLEM

HANLEY

STOKE ON TRENT

SILVERDALE

APEDALE

SLADDERHILL

CHESTERTON

CHATTERLEY (FORMERLY TUNSTALL)

HARECASTLE TUNNELS

TO TALKE & THE NORTH

TO AUDLEY & NANTWICH

SIR NIGEL GRESLEY'S CANAL

APEDALE BRANCH

LONGPORT (FORMERLY BURSLEM)

PORT HILL

TRENT

MERSEY

LIVERPOOL ROAD

QUEEN ST.

NEWCASTLE under LYME JUNCTION CANAL

KNUTTON FORGE

POOL DAM BRANCH

BASFORD

King St.

Brunswick St.

ETRURIA

CANAL

HARTS HILL

TO KEELE & MADELEY

Proposed Inclined Plane

TO MARKET DRAYTON

NEWCASTLE under LYME CANAL

TRENT VALE

TO ECCLESHALL

TO STONE & STAFFORD

(1) POOL DAM SIDINGS
(2) BROOK LANE SIDINGS & BASIN
(3) LIVERPOOL ROAD BASIN
(4) BRAMPTON LEVEL CROSSING AND SIDINGS
(5) STUBBS FIELD BASIN

CANALS

RAILWAYS

ROADS

thence over open land to cross the Lyme Brook by means of a substantial brick culvert, the crumbling remains of which are still to be seen. Veering southwards the canal served a silk mill (erected in 1825 and also surviving in a much modified form) before turning sharply eastwards across Hempstalls Lane and into a cutting, some 400 yards long, which extended as far as King Street. Successive bridges under Queen Street, King Street, Brunswick Street and Hassell Street carried the canal to its terminus in Stubbs Field. The 'inclined plane or railway' would have descended southwards from this point, following the line of the present-day Occupation Street to meet the Newcastle ('Lower') Canal at right angles, but although its construction was under consideration as late as 1831 this essential link was never accomplished. Consequently all three canals suffered from lack of a through route, and the Lower Canal maintained a precarious independence until 1864, when it was vested in the North Staffordshire Railway Company together with its associated 'extension railway', to which reference will be made later. Meanwhile, losses were cut to some extent by the erection and operation of lime burning kilns at the Brook Lane basin, to which limestone was shipped from quarries at Caldon Low via the Caldon branch of the T & M, the product being used as an agricultural fertiliser as well as a fluxing agent in the smelting of iron. The kilns continued to function until the early 1860s, after which they fell into decay. The canal itself gradually became derelict and all through working had ceased by 1920; during the next two decades the entire length — except for about 100 yards at the Stoke end — was abandoned and the stretch alongside London Road at Stoke has been transformed into a public garden.

In 1827 the Gresley family interests passed by marriage into the ownership of Robert Edensor Heathcote and four years later it was he who led a proposal to convert both the Gresley and Junction canals into railways. The renowned George Stephenson was consulted and although he advised that the overall curvature of such a line would be too severe and the cost of an alternative route prohibitive, his report contained details for the construction of the long-awaited inclined plane to connect the basins at Brook Lane and Stubbs Field, though it is evident that the works were never commenced. The Stubbs Field basin was therefore of little use and within a short while permission was obtained for the excavation of an intermediate wharf on a 9,000 sq yds plot lying between King Street and Brunswick Street, bordered on the north side by Water Street. The land formed part of the dwindling Newcastle Marsh, formerly a waterlogged tract of some 23 acres which had been enclosed and drained by a local Act of 1782 and progressively developed as an extension of the town centre. Marsh Parade and Marsh Street (now absorbed into Merrial Street) derived their names from this source and the new wharf in turn became known as Marsh

Wharf. It was to serve as a distributing centre for the Apedale mineral traffic until 1852, thereafter being converted to railway sidings for the same purpose, but for a number of years previously the Brunswick Street-Stubbs Field section of the Junction Canal had been out of use and it was drained in 1851. A short length to the south of Marsh Parade was retained as an engine pond for the nearby silk mill (founded in the early 1820s) and this survived to act as an emergency water supply during World War II; it is marked as a fish pond on the 1878 edition of the Ordnance Survey. In 1905 St Paul's Church was raised across the line of the erstwhile canal and today a bridge parapet in Brunswick Street and the odd alignment of a house wall in West Street are practically the sole reminders of its existence. The advent of the North Staffordshire Railway in 1846 heralded great changes in local transport methods and the later phases of the two Apedale canals were closely concerned with the first stages of the Knotty's Market Drayton branch.

CHAPTER 2

EARLY RAILWAY SCHEMES 1825-1852

Primitive wooden 'railed ways' had been in fairly general use in the vicinity of coal pits and quarries since the beginning of the seventeenth century and in the course of time many of these were converted into iron-plated roads, making for easier haulage and greater durability. The pioneering North Staffordshire industrialists were not unaware of the advantages to be derived from this improved mode of transport and had no doubt noted the action of the proprietors of the Trent & Mersey Canal who, in 1777, obtained parliamentary powers to construct a four-mile long tramroad from the terminus of the Caldon branch canal at Froghall to the limestone quarries 600 ft above. This employment of rails in support of waterways was soon extended to the Potteries district and a number of short feeder lines were laid down from the main canal to nearby factories. The canal owners encouraged the public use of these new railways — on payment of specified rates — and so they became available to any trader whose cart wheels were the right distance apart! It was not long before this method, hitherto regarded merely as a convenient means of transferring canal-borne goods to and from the wharves, was recognised as a much more flexible and a superior form of transportation, and following the success of the Stockton & Darlington enterprise of 1825 the Railway Age had well and truly begun.

So far as Apedale was concerned, much of the coal produced during the eighteenth century had been carried overland to Nantwich, Middlewich and other salt-refining centres in Cheshire, primarily because supplies of charcoal as a heating agent in the evaporation process had become exhausted. The quantities of coal thus consumed were prodigious — as much as two tons of fuel being required to produce three tons of fine salt — and improvements to the River Weaver and the opening of the Chester Canal (in 1779) enabled coal to be shipped from Lancashire pits in preference to the nearer, but less accessible, North Staffordshire coalfield. In an attempt to rebut this unwelcome competition there were renewed plans in 1806 to join the Apedale terminus of Gresley's Canal to the Chester Canal at Nantwich — this time by a tramroad, with a rail connection via Audley to Sneyd's pits and iron works at Silverdale and thence to the 'Lower' Canal at Newcastle. Nothing came of this project (which would have linked the Chester and T & M Canals) but several local colliery lines were built during this period, including one by Walter Sneyd, in 1805, to provide an outlet from his Silverdale works by way of Scot Hay and Leycett to a wharf beside the Newcastle to Nantwich turnpike road at Madeley Heath. The site, just west of the M6 motorway bridge, is still known as 'The Old Wharf' — later this was replaced by a wharf alongside the Leycett colliery line, from which the present-day Wharf Terrace took its name.

The first positive opportunity to provide North Staffordshire with access to the evolving national railway system arose in 1837, when the Grand Junction line was opened between Stafford and Crewe. Unfortunately for local aspirations, but with the object of securing the shortest practicable route to both Liverpool and Manchester as well as taking advantage of the easiest gradients available, the GJR passed no nearer to Newcastle than Whitmore and Madeley, several miles away to the west. From the outset Whitmore was rated as a 'first class' station (at which all trains stopped) in anticipation of its function as a railhead for a wide area, and for a number of years it was served by coaches to and from the Potteries and as far afield as Shrewsbury. The GJR fully intended in time to build a branch line to the Potteries, and their eminent engineer, Joseph Locke, prepared a detailed survey of the route, but there was a considerable delay in furthering the project, due in part to the labour disputes of the early 1840s, when serious rioting broke out in the North Staffordshire towns. By the time the relevant bill was presented to Parliament, in 1845, the North Stafford-shire Railway Company had already been conceived and the Grand Junction's scheme was rejected in favour of the local undertaking. Nevertheless, one Thomas Firmstone, who was then operating the Leycett pits as tenant of Lord Crewe, was quick to avail himself of the new facility and a branch mineral line from Madeley station, some 1½ miles long, was in use by 1840. It was on this line that the 'New Wharf' was built at Madeley Heath. Osborne's *Guide to the Grand Junction Railway* (1838) mentions the enterprising Mr Firmstone and records that he was 'constructing a railroad from his works . . . in order that he may run his own engine and trains to supply the (Railway) Company's stations with coke and to convey iron to Birmingham and Manchester'. Firmstone's engine was at first stabled at Whitmore, on payment to the GJR of a weekly rent of 10s 0d (50p) plus 1s 0d (5p) for each time water was taken, but in later years the colliery company erected its own engine shed beside the main line at Madeley.

Meanwhile, in 1835, a group of North Staffordshire businessmen, headed by Robert Edensor Heathcote, engaged George Stephenson to survey a route for a railway through the district to meet the planned GJR at Norton Bridge. Stephenson's ensuing recommendations in-cluded a branch line from Etruria to 'Heathcote's — formerly Gres-ley's — Canal at or near Newcastle' but the GJR who, as already noted, were formulating their own plans to tap the rich resources of the

Potteries, declined to co-operate and after two years of abortive discussions the entire project was set aside. Eight years later the Railway Mania — 'that remarkable and deplorable spirit of speculation' as the Knotty's chairman was to describe it — was at its height and during 1845 no fewer than sixteen separate proposals for railways to pass through North Staffordshire were under active consideration. Of these, the Derby & Crewe Junction (sponsored by the GJR) and the Churnet Valley (sponsored by the London & Birmingham) were the most significant, but the rival sponsors were soon to join forces and become the London & North Western — leaving the way clear for the formation of the independent North Staffordshire Railway Company. This new company was incorporated by three distinct Acts of Parliament, outlined in the directors' first report to the shareholders as follows:

(i) *The Potteries Line* — from the London & North Western Railway at Macclesfield, through Congleton, the Potteries and Stone, to the Trent Valley portion of the London & North Western Railway at Colwich, with branches to Newcastle-under-Lyme and Norton Bridge.

(ii) *The Churnet Valley Line* — from the London & North Western Railway at Macclesfield (actually North Rode junction) to the Birmingham & Derby line of the Midland Railway at Burton-on-Trent, with a branch from Uttoxeter through the Potteries to Crewe and

(iii) *The Harecastle and Sandbach Line* — from Harecastle on the Potteries line, to Sandbach on the Manchester & Birmingham branch of the London & North Western Railway.

All three Acts received the Royal Assent on 26 June 1846 and this same legislation empowered the NSR to acquire the interests of the Trent & Mersey Navigation, with which it would otherwise have been 'in direct and complete competition'. The canal was purchased for £1,170,000 and as well as gaining the valuable limestone quarries at Caldon Low, the Knotty thus became the third largest canal-owning company in the kingdom, possessing a water mileage of 119 by the year 1900. The three Acts were consolidated by the North Staffordshire Railway Act which received the Royal Assent on 2 July 1847 and contained additional powers for the construction of a branch line beyond Newcastle — 'to terminate at or near certain ironworks belonging to Ralph Sneyd and his lessees'.

The cutting of first sods was a customary adjunct to the inauguration of early railways and the Knotty excelled by arranging two such ceremonies — one at Stoke following the first annual general meeting of the company, on 23 September 1846, and the second at Stone, on the Norton Bridge line, on 11 February 1847. The route to Norton Bridge (where a junction with the LNWR was formed) was ready for traffic just over one year later and by the end of 1849 some 111 miles of double track were open for public use. In contrast to this rapid progress, however, construction of the branch to Newcastle (from Newcastle Junction on the Stoke to Harecastle main line) was not commenced until 1849, for not only was the new company primarily concerned with the speedy establishment of more lucrative links with the Midland and London & North Western Railways, but difficulties had been encountered in the way of land acquisition and the works were interrupted by an Injunction in Chancery. A more substantial cause of delay was the need to pierce the Hartshill-Basford ridge, which straddled the line of route some 100 ft above rail level and which was to involve the driving of two tunnels, 145 and 577 yds in length, separated by a deep cutting about 100 yds long.

The hesitant advance of the promised branch to Newcastle and beyond brought little consolation to Ralph Sneyd, whose business was already suffering the effects of a general recession in trade and who was soon to lease the Silverdale mines and furnaces to his partner, Francis Stanier. Frustrated by the delay and in increasing doubt as to whether the proposed line would ever extend beyond Heathcote's canal, Sneyd set about building a private railway — mainly over his own land — from the ironworks to a wharf at Pool Dam, Newcastle, on the north side of the turnpike road to Keele and close by the site of the medieval 'new castle' — for the defence of which a large pool had been created by damming the River Lyme. Sneyd's so-called Silverdale & Newcastle-under-Lyme Railway was constructed in 1849-50 and in 1853 its usefulness was enhanced by a half-mile extension from Pool Dam to the basin of the Lower Canal at Brook Lane. This 'Canal Extension Railway' was financed and built by the canal company (which was still an independent body) 'for the purpose of facilitating the passage of traffic' and to ensure that the town was 'supplied with coal and ironstone conveyed to and from the said canal'. Curiously, the section from Pool Dam was ordered to be worked 'by horse haulage only' and it was not until 1881 that the then owners (the Knotty) obtained leave to dispense with this hampering stipulation.

The 'Newcastle branch' left the main line at a point about ¼ mile north of Stoke station and ran for a distance of exactly two miles to a station at King Street, Newcastle, the first building being described as 'temporary' as the Knotty prudently decided to 'await the requirements of the public' before erecting a permanent structure on the same site. In the sylvan setting of Station Walks the station amply justified a local newspaper's reference to 'really a most picturesque spot'. At long last the line was inspected and approved by Captain Galton, R.E., and traffic commenced on Monday, 6 September 1852. At the outset, no fewer than fourteen passenger trains ran each way between Newcastle and Stoke, most of them being timed to connect with main line services at the latter place. Six minutes were allowed for the journey, fares being at the rate of 4d (1.4p), 3d (1.25p) and 2d (0.7p) for first, second and third class passengers respectively. Nine trains ran each way on Sundays and certain services were extended beyond Stoke to Longton.

As the new branch neared completion, Ralph Sneyd was quick to approach the NSR with a guarantee of traffic and, accordingly, the line (at first single throughout) was continued to a junction with the S & NR at Knutton. In the previous year (1851) the NSR had purchased the Junction Canal for £1,000 and its bed in the cutting was converted to railway tracks between Hempstalls Lane (also known as Back Brampton) and Newcastle station — a distance of about ¼ mile. At the same time the easterly continuation of the Junction Canal, together with the Marsh Wharf, was also drained and the latter was laid out as a railway goods yard, the eastern part for the Company's general use and the remainder as a depot for Heathcote's Apedale minerals. Additional sidings were provided to the west of Hempstalls Lane ('Brampton sidings') and cattle docks were built here at a later date. The former canal bridge carrying King Street over the single rail track into the goods yard presented a troublesome obstacle to all but the Apedale company's small locomotives as the overhead clearance was only 11ft 8in, compared with the normal NSR loading gauge of 13ft 5in. Of NSR engines, only the long-lived Nos 58A and 59A 0-6-0 saddle tanks (LMS Nos 1600 and 1601) and, possibly, the two Kerr Stuart 0-6-0 tanks Nos 74 and 75 (LMS Nos 1602 and 1603) could safely negotiate this bridge and for many years cable haulage was employed, electrically driven capstans being installed on either approach in about 1900.

Within ten years of the opening, increasing traffic had led to the doubling of the track from Newcastle westwards and shunting operations were further assisted by the laying of a running loop between the station and Brampton level crossing, the former canal cutting being widened to accommodate three tracks. The western part of the goods yard continued to be reserved for the Apedale traffic but when this ceased abruptly in 1930 the land was taken over for non-railway purposes; the very low bridge under Brunswick Street was retained until the 1920s to provide access for rail waggons to a coal merchant's depot, the site having since been occupied by a billiards hall and latterly by a ballroom.

By the end of 1852 "public requirements" had been more accurately assessed and there had been some adjustments to the original time table. The services for December were as follows:

Newcastle to Stoke:
6.50am 8.0am 9.40am+ 11.35am
2.10pm+ 2.50pm 3.55pm 4.30pm+ 5.50pm 7.20pm 7.55pm 8.45pm
(Sundays at 8.35am 10.20am 10.50am
   2.0pm 3.10pm+ 5.50pm 6.30pm 7.50pm 8.35pm)
+ Runs through to Longton.

Stoke to Newcastle:
7.10am 8.30am 10.10am
12.25pm 2.30pm 3.10pm 4.0pm 5.5pm 6.20pm 7.35pm 8.35pm
(Sundays at 8.20am 9.5am 10.40am
   1.30pm 2.20pm 3.35pm 5.10pm 6.50pm 8.25pm)

It had always been intended that the Stoke-Newcastle line would be the means of providing an outlet for the mineral wealth of the Apedale valley, as well as Silverdale, and the 1847 Act made specific reference to the construction of a rail connection throughout. The extension to Knutton Junction hastened the building of the Apedale branch and this 1½ mile long single line, curving away north-westwards from Apedale Junction (via Knutton Gate) was officially opened in November 1853 — simultaneously with the Marsh Wharf sidings. The new branch effectively replaced both the Gresley and Junction Canals and in return for an indemnity against any interference with waterborne traffic during the period of construction, Heathcote undertook to hand over the remaining canal sections to the NSR within seven days of the railway's completion. The NSR subsequently leased these sections to Francis Stanier (Heathcote's successor) and in order to maintain the terms of the lease Stanier shipped two barge loads of coal from Apedale to the Cross Heath cotton mill on the first and last days of each year. This arrangement lapsed on the formation of the Midland Coal, Coke & Iron Company in January 1890 and much of the canal thereafter became derelict, although the new owners utilised the water as a cooling agent at the ironworks by means of an ingenious re-cycling system. It seems that NSR workings over the branch preceded the official opening date by several months, for the company's records show that in July 1853 thrice-weekly trains of iron began running from the Whitebarn sidings, on the southern fringe of Apedale, to Parker's main works at Bloomfield (Tipton) in South Staffordshire — via Stoke and Stone, LNWR locomotives taking over at Norton Bridge. Following the advent of the railway, the valley became threaded by a network of lines and sidings serving a complex of various commercial activities, including chemical works, a brick yard and waggon repair shops. At the peak of its prosperity over 3,000 workpeople were employed in the valley — chiefly from the Chesterton area, whose population almost doubled to just under 10,000 between 1871 and 1901 — but unlike industrial valleys elsewhere, no long terraces of workers' dwellings were ever built in Apedale; the value of the land outweighed the advantage of having a source of labour close at hand.

The Whitebarn sidings diverged from the Apedale branch at a junction near Hooters Hall Farm and continued south-westwards to service a group of small mines before joining the Knutton to Silverdale line (S & NR) at Grove Junction. These mines included the Oak, Knutton Farm, Grove and Gorsty Bank, all of which had been abandoned by 1895 after a brief but prosperous existence. In 1857 Francis Stanier and his partners set up a forge at Knutton, on the south side of the S & NR and it was therefore desirable to obtain formal running powers for the Apedale company's locomotives and trains over the Apedale Junction-Knutton Junction section as well as to the Marsh Wharf. These powers were granted by the NSR for an annual fee of £500 and so began the regular working of privately-owned trains over this part of the Knotty's system — to be followed by those of the Silverdale company — a practice which was to become common throughout North Staffordshire and a convenient source of revenue for the NSR.

CHAPTER 3

DEVELOPMENT 1852-1865

For several years after 1852 the NSR branch from Stoke rested in the arms of Sneyd's railway at Knutton Junction. Its position was far from being secure, for away towards the Welsh Marches hostile forces were already gathering which would attack the Knotty's outlying defences more than once during the next two decades. These attacks would be focussed upon the small country town of Market Drayton, which was without a railway of any kind until 1863, although there had been plans to replace the nearby canal by a railway some eighteen years before. This proposal was put forward at the height of the Railway Mania, when the newly constituted Shropshire Union Canal company (formerly Telford's Birmingham & Liverpool Junction) launched a scheme to convert the canal between its terminus at Wolverhampton and Calverley, in Cheshire, where a connection was to be made with the Chester & Crewe Railway. The proposal was supported by the London & Birmingham Railway as a means of challenging the GJR's hold on the North-West, but the closing months of 1845 witnessed a sudden and dramatic change in the policies of these two companies and in the following July they united (with the lesser Manchester & Birmingham) to form the mighty London & North Western Railway Company — who promptly leased the canal!

Set in the midst of an area remarkably devoid of railways, bounded by the Potteries, Stafford, Wellington and Nantwich, Market Drayton presented an obvious target for further expansion, and by the early 1860s the commercial possibilities of lines between Shrewsbury and the Potteries and between Wellington and Crewe were to guarantee its place as a potential railway centre of some importance. Meanwhile, it was not surprising that the aspiring LNWR regarded the development of the North Staffordshire Railway system with something less than equanimity. In due course a rather uneasy working agreement on the movement of through traffic was drawn up by the LNWR and NSR, but the burgeoning wealth of North Staffordshire remained susceptible to exploitation — primarily by the North Western, but also by that company's arch-rival, the Great Western, who would have dearly loved to reach the Potteries as a stepping stone to the rich prize of Manchester. Relationships with the LNWR sank to their lowest ebb during this period; the smaller company in August 1858 went so far as to transfer the bulk of its London traffic from the LNWR at Colwich to the Midland and Great Northern Railways via Derby. The North

Western at once retaliated, not only by augmenting its agencies in the Potteries towns and arranging for the intensified cartage of goods to and from Whitmore station (thus avoiding NSR dues) but — more threateningly — by commencing a survey for a line of its own from either Whitmore or Madeley into North Staffordshire, a revival of the old Grand Junction scheme. This new prospect of a rail link that would free them from the 'monopolistic' freight charges of the Knotty and its canal found much favour with the pottery manufacturers but the departure in 1858 of the General Manager, Mark Huish, led to an improvement in the working arrangements with the NSR, though not before the LNWR had made its last overt thrust at the Knotty (in 1859) by lending support to the ambitious Shrewsbury & Potteries Junction project. A more substantial contract was reached in August 1860, which was hailed by the Knotty's board of directors as 'a treaty of peace'. Having just absorbed the South Staffordshire Railway (and thereby shattering the Knotty's dream of a link with the Great Western system by way of Colwich, Cannock and Wednesbury) perhaps the LNWR could afford to be magnanimous! The ill-fated Shrewsbury & Potteries Junction proposal was to recur in various guises over the years, as will be noted, but on this occasion the day was saved by Sneyd's successful application to make the S & NR a public concern, whereupon the NSR (whose chairman had described the North Western's intrigues as 'the thin end of the wedge') vigorously opposed the enemy bill in Parliament, who ruled in favour of the North Staffordshire company.

The Silverdale & Newcastle Railway was made public by an Act dated 13 August 1859. This was not Sneyd's only venture, for during the 1850s he and his lessees had built another private line from Chatterley sidings (Tunstall) on the NSR's main route, to the collieries at Talke. The value — both economic and strategic — of this independent rail network was clearly recognised by the Knotty who, foreseeing further incursions from the west, took urgent steps to acquire the whole of Sneyd's railway interests. The North Staffordshire Railway Act of 1860 authorised a 999-years lease of the S & NR and on 31 August that year a contract was signed whereby Ralph Sneyd and his successors undertook not to allow the use of his railways by or in connection with any public company other than the NSR. The line to Silverdale was opened for minerals in 1861 and from this date the S & NR eastwards from Knutton Junction became known as the Pool Dam branch, collectively with the Canal Extension Railway. The completion of the Stoke-Silverdale rail link led to a gradual abandonment of the Lower Canal, but the branch provided a useful freight service until its closure in October 1967. At one time or another it catered for the Castle Hill iron foundry, two coal wharves, a brewery (reached by a short spur to Lower Street) and the Corporation gas works, which were erected alongside the Extension line in 1855. The building of the iron foundry, also in 1855, seriously disturbed the site of the castle, of which only a small excavated portion is now visible.

The continuation of the branch from the Pool Dam wharf to the Brook Lane canal basin necessitated three level crossings — all of main highways to and from the town centre — and shunting activities, although infrequent and under the control of a flagman, gave rise to annoying interference with road traffic, especially during the last years of operation.

In 1851 Ralph Sneyd (who was intent on re-building Keele Hall) had handed over the management of the Silverdale mines and ironworks to his partner, Francis Stanier, who died at Madeley Manor in October 1856. Stanier's son, also Francis, took over on attaining his majority in 1858 and a period of comparative prosperity began, during which the Apedale works were incorporated (in 1864) and extended. Sneyd died a bachelor in July 1870, at the age of 77 and was succeeded by his brother, the Reverend Walter Sneyd. When Walter died in 1888, the estate passed to his 25 years old son (another Ralph) who was destined to witness the end of his family's long association with the industrial history of North Staffordshire.

The Knotty's western defences were now augmented by the laying of a second line of rails on the north side of the former S & NR from Knutton Junction into Silverdale — a distance of about one mile — and this was opened for mineral traffic in 1861 and for passengers two years later. In 1859 a bill for the construction of a short branch from Knutton Junction to Knutton village had been rejected and the inhabitants had to await the opening of Knutton halt in 1905. The first station to serve the growing community of Silverdale (its population increased from 933 in 1831 to 6,383 in 1871) was sited on the south side of the line, just short of St Luke's Church which had been erected in 1853 on land donated by Ralph Sneyd. The original station master's house at No 151 Church Street was one of a group of stone-built Victorian Gothic cottages raised by Sneyd, now replaced by modern dwellings. Hereabouts Sneyd's railway veered away to the north-west to service his ironworks, marking the beginning of the pre-1870 branch to Leycett and Audley and known as 'the cuttings' because of the extensive excavations required. In 1858 the NSR had attempted to gain access to the Audley area by a northwards extension of the Apedale branch, but this was vetoed by Heathcote on the grounds that trains would pass uncomfortably close to his residence at Apedale Hall. Instead, parliamentary powers to build a branch from the proposed Market Drayton line at Honeywall (Keele) to Leycett were included in the 'New Works' Act of 1864.

The early 1860s witnessed a minor revival of railway mania and during this period two separate undertakings, designed to meet end-on at Market Drayton, had been incorporated, namely, the Nantwich & Market Drayton (10¾ miles) in June 1861 and the Wellington & Drayton (15½ miles) in August 1862. The N & MDR had been promoted by a group of local gentry and landowners, headed by Mr Henry Reginald Corbet, of Adderley Hall and the line ran from a junction with the Shrewsbury & Crewe Railway at Nantwich to a terminus just short of the Adderley road at Market Drayton, closely following the Shropshire Union Canal for much of the way. In November 1861 the same promoters deposited plans for a second railway to run from Market Drayton to join the Stafford-Wellington (Shropshire Union) line at Newport, but despite the interest shown in the venture by the Duke of Sutherland (who owned the collieries surrounding his Lilleshall estate) this project did not materialise. Like the Shrewsbury & Crewe at that time, the N & MDR was built as a single track. The opening ceremony, on 19 October 1863, proved to be an event of considerable local importance, the celebrations including a grand procession through the garlanded streets of Drayton and two days of feasting and general merrymaking.

The Wellington & Drayton Railway was the remaining stump of the more impressive Wellington & Cheshire Junction, which was aimed at Northwich and Manchester — and for that reason fostered by the GWR. Its route into Cheshire overlapped that of the Nantwich & Market Drayton and understandably incurred the wrath of both the LNWR and the NSR, who successfully opposed the full scheme. Nevertheless, the W & DR's incorporation in 1862 encouraged the Shrewsbury & Potteries Junction to re-enter the lists, this time with the forceful backing of the Great Western. Significantly, strong support was also forthcoming from the influential Potteries Chamber of Commerce, whose members had long smarted under the 'exorbitant rates' imposed by the NSR and its affiliated canal, which together held a virtual monopoly on the transport of goods in that district. At a public meeting in Hanley, on 17 February 1862, favourable consideration was given to the prospectus of the new line which, it was explained, would run from the neighbourhood of Market Drayton to Madeley (where a double junction with the LNWR was envisaged) and thence to Silverdale 'where it would join the present line to Newcastle and the Potteries'. A packed audience, including many leading pottery manufacturers, loudly applauded the promise of a railway that would enable china clay to be transported direct from Dorset, thus avoiding the circuitous route by water — as well as the Knotty's canal dues! A case was quoted of a London dealer who received two invoices for identical goods, one from Yorkshire (200 miles) at 16 shillings (80p) per ton and one from North Staffordshire (50 miles nearer) for which he had to pay 35 shillings (£1.75p) owing to the Knotty's extortionate charges. Two years and much wrangling later the Knotty was forced to reduce its canal tolls to defeat the latest and most determined attack by the S & PJR, as will be noted. As it was, the 1862 venture, which appeared to assume that running powers over the Knotty's Silverdale line would be granted as a matter of course, met with predictable opposition from the NSR — with whom the LNWR again joined forces — and after a 'severe battle' the bill was defeated in the House of Lords, their Lordships expressing the view that if a line to Market Drayton was to be built it ought to be entrusted to the North Staffordshire company, who had already 'invested a large capital for the accommodation of the district'.

Undaunted, the S & PJR set to work on a new prospectus — this time with an independent route of its own into the Potteries. The revised scheme of 1863-4 comprised a line from the Shrewsbury & Crewe at Harlescott (just north of the county town) and thence via Shawbury to a junction with the authorised W & DR between Hodnet and Market Drayton. A new and complex system of proposed running powers in the Shrewsbury area involved connections with the Wellington, Severn Valley, Hereford and Weshpool lines, together with use of the General station — this last was refused by Parliament at the behest of the LNWR/GWR joint ownership, resulting in a deviation from the Welshpool line at Red Hill (some three miles out of Shrewsbury) and the building of a spur to a separate terminus at Abbey Foregate — Shrewsbury's 'other station'. Eastwards from Market Drayton a great sweep was planned by way of Madeley, Audley, Harecastle, Tunstall and Burslem to a terminus off Etruria Road at Hanley, to which town the Knotty had opened a goods line (the first stage of the famous 'Loop Line') in December 1861 and which seemed to the frustrated inhabitants of Burslem and Tunstall to mark the limit of the NSR's intentions in their direction. The track was to be doubled between Tunstall and Hanley — over which 'a large passenger traffic' was expected — and the Hanley terminus would be immediately opposite, but not physically linked, to that of the Knotty. The Tunstall-Market Drayton section of just under 20 miles was to be single-track, with a ruling gradient of 1 in 100 and while tunnels were to be avoided, very extensive cuttings and embankments would be necessary, the cost of this section being estimated at £316,604. A number of off-shoots would serve collieries and ironworks en route — including the Clough Hall works at Kidsgrove — and junctions were to be formed with Sneyd's Talke/Jamage line and, more importantly, with the LNWR at the crossing point between Wrinehill and Betley. However, the branch most relevant to the present history was that planned to run from Halmerend to a junction with the NSR at Newcastle station, which the S & PJR sought authority to use 'together with its approaches, water supply, water engines, sidings, machinery, works and conveniences'. Impelled by the audacity of this proposed invasion of their territory, the Knotty's directors — having no doubt taken to heart the recent advice of the House of Lords — announced their conclusion that 'it was impossible any longer to resist the claims of the Drayton district to the communication they had long sought with the Potteries'. Consequently, the company had found it prudent to prepare a scheme of its own and, as the chairman put it, 'not being anxious to go beyond our own district which is bounded on the west by the London & North Western Railway' it was proposed that the LNWR should build the line from Market Drayton to Madeley, from where the NSR would proceed to an end-on junction with the existing railway at Silverdale. Alternatively, it was suggested that the Drayton-Madeley section should be a joint undertaking but the LNWR declined to adopt either proposition and the Knotty was left 'to go it alone'. Moreover, at the half-yearly meeting of NSR shareholders on 10 February 1864, the chairman referred to the proposed extension from Silverdale to the N & MDR and revealed that to the original plan had been added 'lines for developing the districts of Chesterton, Audley and other places which, it was well known, were exceedingly rich in coal and ironstone — two of the three great elements in the manufacture of iron'. It was recognised that these resources had been only partially exploited and railway communication was required to develop them fully and satisfactorily. A 'network of lines' had therefore been designed, with the sanction of the various landowners concerned and 'all would be connected with the existing lines'. Thus were born the 'New Works' and 'Branches' Acts of 1864 and the bills as finally presented to Parliament requested authority (a) to lease or purchase Sneyd's Talke railway and to extend it to the collieries at Bignall Hill (b) to build additional lines from Chatterley to Chesterton and into Tunstall and Burslem (all from the Stoke-Harecastle main line) and (c) to construct a line from Silverdale to Alsager (the original Audley branch via 'the cuttings') with connections to the Diglake (Audley), Bignall Hill and Jamage collieries — the last-named being close to the terminus of Sneyd's Talke railway. The Silverdale-Market Drayton section was to include a link with the LNWR about one mile south of that company's Madeley station and a short spur from Honeywall (west of the proposed station at Keele) to the Audley branch at Leycett — both junctions to face westwards in the direction of Market Drayton. A 'network of lines' indeed — and one designed to encompass the whole of the Audley-Apedale-Chesterton coalfield and safeguard the area from any would-be invader, notably the S & PJR!

The Shropshire company quickly parried this move by expressing their determination to gain running powers 'over so much of the respective railways to be authorised by the North Staffordshire Railway (Branches and New Works) Acts as will lie between Market Drayton and Audley' and it is clear that the promoters were encouraged by the growing hostility of local businessmen to the NSR, as crystalised in the Potteries Chamber of Commerce, to whom the Knotty's chairman in a contemporary report to the shareholders referred bitterly as 'this third party . . . who have given us so much trouble and put us to so much expense'. The long delay in extending the Loop Line gave rise to a number of public meetings, at one of which the Town Clerk of Hanley expressed the hope that his town 'would go heart and soul with the other opposing bodies to teach a lesson to the North Staffordshire Railway, which had played fast and loose with them (the corporation) for so long . . . whether the line profitable or not, the NSR had voluntarily offered to make it and they should be compelled to keep their promise'. Joining the fray, the *Staffordshire Sentinel* commented, with some heat: 'The main line (of the NSR) was projected to accommodate the Pottery towns and yet it was insanely laid out as if to avoid them. The line should have avoided the Harecastle tunnels and the valley of fields and should have come through Kidsgrove, Tunstall, Burslem, Cobridge, Hanley and Stoke, but it shuns five out of six of those places as though it wanted not their traffic and was blind to their interests and to its own.'

Support for the S & PJR was also found among the Newcastle Borough Council, although some members warned that the proposed route into the town from Halmerend would seriously encroach upon the public gardens alongside the northern edge of the Junction Canal cutting in which the Knotty's line to Knutton had been laid over ten years previously. These gardens, or 'walks', which link Hempstalls Lane with King Street were developed as the result of an Inclosure Act of 1816; they are still in existence and continue to be known as 'Station Walks' although their namesake has disappeared without trace.

The situation was again critical for the Knotty as the rival schemes went before Parliament. Initially, the House of Commons committee had given preference to the S & PJR on the ground that it had been first in the field, but the Lords, once more showing their confidence in the 'native' company, overthrew the recommendation of the lower House while making it clear that the NSR should take urgent steps to re-introduce its bills to the next session. To this the North Staffordshire directors agreed readily enough, and after some demur the S & PJR consented to withdraw from the scene, on the understanding that its eastern goal would thenceforward be set at Market Drayton, from where running powers of the NSR's future branch to Silverdale and Stoke-on-Trent were promised. The Potteries Chamber of Commerce were openly delighted with this 'compromise' and it is apparent that the Knotty was able to carry the day only by implementing quite substantial cuts in its canal tolls on earthenware and materials, this being the price exacted by the pottery manufacturers for renouncing their support for the Shropshire company. In succeeding years the 'exceptionally low' dividends (3 to 3½%) were publicly attributed by the Knotty's chairman to this 'compulsory sacrifice' — which, however, he considered had been justified by 'the threat of competing lines through the most vulnerable part of our frontier, the Silverdale district'. The enabling Acts were ratified on 29 July 1864 and Market Drayton's third railway was thus given the 'right away'.

Meanwhile, it seems that the original Stoke to Silverdale section of the branch was working satisfactorily and profitably. The majority of the passenger services still terminated at Newcastle, but four trains ran on to Silverdale each weekday (three on Sundays) and there was a morning and evening through working between Newcastle and Longton. In September 1868 an excursion train was run from Silverdale to Rhyl which consisted of '40 coaches and vans' — no doubt all four-wheelers; the number of locomotives is not known!

On 16 January 1866 an accident occurred which had all the makings of a disaster. In the early afternoon a goods train left Stoke for Silverdale with a banking engine at the rear, and as some shunting had to be done at Newcastle the long line of waggons was brought to a standstill in the cutting to the east of the station. Before the shunting had been completed, the 1.28pm ex-Stoke passenger train emerged from the tunnel and struck the banking engine; a number of passengers were badly shaken but no one was seriously hurt. In its report on the incident, the *Staffordshire Advertiser* remarked:

'It is said that no blame is attached to the driver of the passenger train. On the contrary, his collectedness and promptitude no doubt prevented the accident from being more serious, but great carelessness was manifested by someone in charge of the signals, who should have kept the line clear until the arrival of the train at the station.'

It is not known whether the block telegraph had been installed on the branch at this time (the NSR first adopted the system in 1863) but, if so, it was not being operated correctly on this occasion.

The 1865 time table for the branch was as follows:

DOWN
Stoke to Newcastle: 6.40am (ex-Longton) 10.08am 11.00am
12.15pm 3.25pm 4.30pm 5.25pm and 9.25pm
(Sundays at 8.40pm)
Stoke-Newcastle-Silverdale: 8.05am (ex-Longton) 1.28pm 6.25pm and 7.25pm
(Sundays at 9.20am 1.30pm and 7.20pm)

UP
Silverdale-Newcastle-Stoke: 9.10am 2.30pm 6.45pm and 7.55pm (to Longton)
(Sundays at 10.20am 1.50pm and 7.45pm)
Newcastle to Stoke: 7.05am (to Longton) 10.18am 12.40pm 4.10pm 4.40pm 5.50pm
and 9.40pm
(Sundays at 8.55pm)

CHAPTER 4

WESTWARDS FROM STOKE

In July 1865 the S & PJR amalgamated with the Shrewsbury & North Wales Railway, which had its origins in the limestone quarries at Llanymynech and which, having failed to obtain running powers over the Shrewsbury & Welshpool into Shrewsbury general station, established its own terminus at Abbey Foregate on the south side of the River Severn. The new combination adopted the title 'Potteries, Shrewsbury & North Wales Railway' — or merely 'The Potts' to an older generation of Salopians. All thoughts of extensive running powers in and around the county town were now abandoned and efforts were concentrated on a direct line to Market Drayton from the neighbourhood of Abbey Foregate. In a fresh mood of hopefulness the 'North Wales' section between Llanymynech and Shrewsbury was opened for all traffic in August 1866 and in noting this event the *Staffordshire Sentinel* reported, with mistaken foresight: 'The Potteries section of the line, which terminates at Market Drayton, there forming a junction with the North Staffordshire Railway, is at present in course of construction and when complete will, with the aid of the Cambrian Railways . . . bring the South Wales district into direct communication with the Potteries.' Unfortunately, the eastwards extension never progressed beyond the outskirts of Shrewsbury town and the PS & NWR soon went into a slow but sure decline until, in June 1880, the Board of Trade closed the line because of the dilapidated state of the track. Years of further dereliction followed but the NSR, at least, retained some belief in its potential, for in 1885 the Knotty's engineer, William Henry Stubbs, was instructed to make a special survey of the entire line as well as the proposed route between Shrewsbury and Market Drayton. In his ensuing report, Stubbs estimated that the cost of renovation would be approximately £71,000 ('which might be reduced if the main line were worked for passenger traffic') and for a single track extension to Drayton — with intermediate stations at Drakeley Heath and Shawbury — a further £100,000. Stubbs expressed his opinion that the proposed line passed through 'rather more fruitful country than our own Market Drayton railway' (!) Prudence prevailed, however, and NSR locomotives were never to be seen at Llanymynech, although it so happened that many years later three ex-NSR four-wheeled coaches would form part of the rolling stock on the line. In 1888 the PS & NWR was revived as the 'Shropshire Railways' whose primary purpose was to construct a line from

Shrewsbury to Hodnet, with onward running powers over the GWR and NSR to Market Drayton and Stoke. Once again ill luck dogged the project and despite the granting of extra time all work ceased in 1891, the company relapsing into renewed lethargy. The promoters no doubt found it galling to note that the proposed 'Potteries' route appeared on several railway maps of the period, including that of the evolving Great Central as late as 1898. In April 1911 the ailing concern was re-formed yet again to become the Shropshire & Montgomeryshire Light Railway under the auspices of Colonel H F Stephens, doyen of so many similar enterprises, and in 1918 he was co-promoter of one last attempt to build a line from Abbey Foregate 'to the North Staffordshire Railway near Market Drayton'.

Another 'also ran' appeared upon the scene during the parliamentary session of 1863-4. This was the Drayton Junction Railway, sponsored by the proprietors of the future Wrexham, Mold & Connah's Quay company, who were planning an extension of their small empire from Wrexham to Whitchurch. The DJR would have run from a triangular junction at Prees (near Whitchurch) on the Shrewsbury to Crewe line of the LNWR, through the villages of Ightfield and Moreton Saye into the newly built (N & MDR) station at Market Drayton — and out again in a sweeping double curve, of two furlongs radius, to cross the Shropshire Union Canal near the turnpike road to Newcastle. From this point the route lay over some eighteen miles of open country to the west of Eccleshall, terminating in a junction with the Stafford-Wellington line (leased by the LNWR) just short of Stafford station, having followed the western side of the LNWR main line southwards from Great Bridgeford. There was to be a spur from the neighbourhood of the latter place to Norton Bridge, whence access could be gained to the NSR's existing line to Stone and Stoke. Early in 1866, further plans were deposited for an extension of the DJR from Stafford to Cannock Chase, with the object of tapping the coalfield around Norton Canes and a petition was raised in the county town in favour of the line which, it was considered, 'will prove advantageous to the town, particularly in facilitating the supply of coal'. Not surprisingly, the DJR scheme was strongly opposed by both the LNWR and GWR (the last named representing the N & MDR and the now authorised W & DR) and eventually its bill was thrown out and no part built, but it is believed that the 'Railway Inn' near Eccleshall was so named in anticipation of the line's construction. Eccleshall itself was dismissed by the opposition as 'a small place which would never pay if a large expenditure upon it were made for railway occupation' and Norton Bridge remains today as its nearest railhead.

Other 'paper railways' of the period included the Sheffield, Shrewsbury & South Wales Direct (via Market Drayton!) the West Midland, another Potteries Junction (from the Shrewsbury & Chester at a point between Pulford and Dodleston, through Whitchurch and Market Drayton to Newcastle — with a branch from Pipe Gate to Harecastle) and, as late as 1872, the Birkenhead, North Wales & Stafford, a revised version of the erstwhile DJR, which was planned to run from the neighbourhood of Wrexham to the newly-established NSR branch at Market Drayton and thence to a double junction with the Stafford & Uttoxeter (opened in December 1867) at Stafford. Had all these schemes materialised, Market Drayton would have rivalled Crewe as the most important railway centre for many miles around!

The close of the 1860s witnessed the end of the second Railway Mania, but also saw the completion of the two surviving railways to Market Drayton, namely, the Wellington & Drayton and the Knotty's line from Silverdale. The contract for the former was let to the renowned Thomas Brassey and in due course connection was made with the N & MDR by an end-on junction just to the west of Market Drayton station; a level crossing was avoided by raising the Adderley road to an overbridge. To facilitate through working the N & MDR was converted to double track and some costly improvements were ordered by the inspecting officer (Colonel Yolland) who pointed out that what had been originated as a branch line was about to form 'a link in a narrow gauge main line between London and Manchester' and that the GWR to the south and the LNWR to the north were laid with much superior track. Additional works included the strengthening of all underbridges and improved interlocking of points and signals — a 'distant signal' being required at Nantwich Junction. The Colonel also stipulated that the 'goods lines' at Market Drayton and Audlem were to be led into 'blind sidings' and ground signals for all facing points should be installed. Thomas Brassey gained the relevant contract — in excess of £42,000 — for which extra capital had to be raised.

The commissioning of the W & DR suffered a last minute postponement by the Board of Trade, who decided (in August 1867) that heavier rail chairs must be used and the official opening on 16 October was rather a tame affair, falling far short of the scale of the N & MDR's launching just four years previously. The *Advertiser* reported, somewhat crisply:

'This short line was opened on Wednesday after many delays which have tried the patience of the neighbourhood. There was little display or public rejoicing on this occasion, but the ultimate usefulness and prosperity of the enterprise must not on that account be slightly spoken of. The line will be important to the Great Western Company as giving them direct communication through Nantwich and Crewe with the Potteries, Manchester and the North. It will give the people of the district both increased facilities for distant journeys North and South and those aids to communication with neighbouring districts by which their resources will be developed and turned to the best advantage.'

The stated object of the 1864 North Staffordshire Railway (Silverdale, Madeley and Drayton) Act was to authorise the construction of railways from Silverdale 'to the old manor house at Madeley and thence to the Nantwich & Market Drayton and London & North Western Railways'. In contrast to the activity of the preceding Parliamentary stages, progress was slow, and five and a half years were to elapse before the first passengers could take advantage of the new 'communication' — potential travellers on the Audley branch were destined to wait almost three times as long! Apart from two tunnels (between Silverdale and Keele and at Ridgehill, west of Honeywall Junction) and the crossing of the LNWR main line there do not seem to have been any outstanding problems; on the other hand, the line from Silverdale to Leycett entailed the excavation of a long, deep cutting succeeded by a high embankment and this two-miles section was susceptible from the outset to mining subsidence and flooding. Sneyd's ironworks were at first served by a steeply graded back shunt from the so-called 'cuttings', but this troublesome section was abandoned soon after the alternative route between Honeywall and Leycett became available, in July 1870, and the ironworks were thereafter linked with the Market Drayton branch through the colliery sidings. 'The cuttings' — bereft of rail tracks since the 1880s — long remained a well-defined feature of the landscape and only in recent years has repeated tipping of colliery waste and other spoil begun to restore the original contours.

In December 1865 the contract was let to William Field, of Shrewsbury, who had assisted Brassey in building the W & DR. Few details of the construction have come to light but the labour force appear to have conducted themselves well; in January 1868 a local newspaper, referring to Norton-in-Hales, reported that 'the quiet of this little village (has been) uninterrupted by a year's sojourn of navvies located in it.' Methods had scarcely advanced from the pick-and-shovel age and in 1867 two fatal accidents occurred involving the use of horse-drawn tip waggons. The works proceeded against a sombre backcloth of economic depression, particularly in the iron trade, on which the Company so much depended, and the financial expediency of amalgamation with the LNWR was broached on more than one occasion. At the half-yearly meeting of shareholders in June 1867, hopes were expressed that the recently-revised traffic arrangements with the LNWR would be beneficial — through train working by the North Western over NSR metals was due to come into operation that September and the major company had agreed to take out of service 'certain trains that were in opposition to North Staffordshire interests'. The Knotty's chairman expressed his belief that the two companies 'would henceforward work in perfect amity, great pains having been taken to prevent future disputes'. In his *History of the London & North Western Railway* (1914) W L Steel commented upon this 'very important agreement' as follows:

'. . . It was realised that the interests of both companies would be best served by a system of close working and since the attempts at amalgamation had previously proved abortive, it was arranged to enter into a new working agreement (which was) an excellent one for both parties. To the North Western it meant that should the North Stafford ever become hostile, or by any chance fall into other hands, the North Western would still have access to the important district of the Potteries with its own trains and would still be able to make use of the North Stafford as a link in its chain of communication.'

Urged on by the Chamber of Commerce, authority for the Loop Line extension beyond Hanley had been obtained in July 1865 but two years later the worsening trade situation prompted the Knotty to seek parliamentary sanction to abandon this future money-spinner, together with the Tunstall and Burslem spur lines already mentioned. Not surprisingly, local voices were again raised in vehement protest and the only concession was for an extension of time to complete the works. However, no such easement was allowed in the case of the Market Drayton and Audley branches, though there was talk of reducing them both to a single track — an economy that was to be adopted some sixty years later! On the Drayton line the company's engineer (J C Forsyth) encountered what he described as 'excessive demands' for land compensation — which were perhaps to be expected in such a rich agricultural district — and numerous accommodation bridges and crossings had to be provided for farmers whose fields were being broken up by the new railway. In all, the 12½ miles section from Silverdale to the junction with the N & MDR contained 29 bridges and 27 level crossings, three of the latter being manned — at Silverdale by the station signalman and at Knighton and Betton Moss by resident keepers. The Knotty's finances continued at a low ebb and at least one shareholder blamed 'the miserable Silverdale and Market Drayton line, which is one chief cause of our trouble' and further alleged that the company would never have embarked upon its construction 'were it not for the interests of the (T & M) canal'. Nevertheless, at the half-yearly meeting on 11 August 1868, the chairman was able to confirm that the estimates for the line had proved to be 'pretty correct' and he went on to explain that the directors had not 'pressed these works forward as much as they might have done because the preference stock was not taken up as they wished and much of it was obliged to be sold at a discount'. [A capital sum of £175,000 had been allowed, with loans amounting to £58,000. The actual cost was about £217,000.] They were unwilling to sell more than they could help but it now seemed desirable to make a special effort 'when so much money is lying idle'. Six months later, at the 46th Annual General Meeting, shareholders were informed that the New Works, which had so long been retarded by the difficulty in raising capital, were now making rapid progress. In response to renewed pressure for a union with the LNWR, the chairman pointed out that the terms so far suggested had been unacceptable — in the belief that a more favourable offer might be forthcoming once traffic on the Audley and Market Drayton branches had developed!

The excavations west of Silverdale station laid bare certain geological features which indicated that workable coal measures extended into eastern Shropshire and this discovery was of particular interest to Mr Corbet of Adderley (Chairman of the N & MDR) who, among many other pursuits, was at that time carrying out trial borings for coal at Childs Ercall, six miles south of Market Drayton. Fortunately, that pleasant countryside was to be spared the unsightliness of industrial development — unlike Silverdale, lamented as a pleasing pastoral, undulating vale, with fair fields through which meandered a pure, cheerful stream . . ." formerly. A street in Silverdale was named 'Vale Pleasant' — no doubt in remembrance of those more idyllic days and, all in all, it would seem that Ralph Sneyd and his successors had much to answer for!

The line from Silverdale to Market Drayton (Silverdale Junction) was inspected by Colonel Yolland on Thursday 27 January 1870. The *Staffordshire Advertiser* reported: 'The result of the examination was satisfactory and the Directors announce that the line will be opened on Tuesday next. There will be stations at Market Drayton, Norton-in-Hales, Pipe Gate (for Pipe Gate and Woore) and Keele (for Keele and Madeley). Four trains will run daily each way on weekdays and two on Sundays and the journey from Stoke to Market Drayton will occupy three quarters of an hour. The new line will bring the fertile agricultural district of North Shropshire into direct communication with the teeming population of the Potteries with, it is anticipated, results beneficial to the inhabitants of both districts. But not only will the railway give our Salopian neighbours facilities of access to a profitable market for their commodities, but it will also tend to the further development of the mineral resources of North Staffordshire. For example, there is an accommodation line at Silverdale which runs through to the Leycett colliery, worked by the Leycett & Crewe Colliery Company, who have for mining purposes leased upwards of 4,000 acres from Lord Crewe . . . it also brings North Staffordshire into direct communication with the Great Western system, a condition of affairs which may in the process of time prove to be advantageous to the district.' (This 'accommodation line' was intended to form the main route to Halmerend and Audley; the line from Leycett to Honeywall was to be a minor branch.)

The official opening for both goods and passengers duly took place on Tuesday 1 February 1870. As had been the case of the W & DR, there were no widespread junketings to mark the occasion although a commemorative Public Ball was held in the Corbet Arms assembly rooms (Market Drayton) on 17 February, and the *Sentinel* of 19

February contained the following paragraph: 'On Wednesday night, by way of celebrating the opening of the line, there was a dinner at the Chetwynd (actually Chetwode) Arms Inn, Pipe Gate. About thirty sat down, including several Silverdale visitors. A beautiful spread was provided . . . Mr Goodall of Silverdale, the Chairman, suitably proposed the Loyal Toasts. Mr Williams, stationmaster at Silverdale, proposed the toast of "Success to the North Staffordshire Railway Company" . . . a number of toasts were proposed and several gentlemen of the party spoke of the convenience which the locality would enjoy by the running of trains along the new line . . . there was an intermixture of complimentary toasts and the company spent some time pleasantly together.' As the last train to the Potteries left Pipe Gate station at 8.35pm one may assume — from the number of toasts to be honoured — that Mr Goodall and his Silverdale colleagues had travelled by road; or perhaps the company stayed 'pleasantly together' and caught the 10.45 next morning?

There was at least one other celebration. Recently, Mr J S Furnival, of Bearstone, informed the writer that his great-uncle, Mr John Eardley, a farmer at Norton-in-Hales, together with three kindred spirits, drove by pony and trap to Newcastle (about 12 miles) in time to catch the very first passenger train to Market Drayton. After suitable refreshment they caught the next train back — and after further refreshment returned home, no doubt flushed with success!

The extension of the branch from Silverdale necessitated an overall revision of the passenger services to and from Stoke and from February (1870) trains ran as follows:

	DOWN
Stoke to Market Drayton:	9.10am 12.35pm 4.50pm and 7.25pm
	Sundays at 9.00am and 7.20pm)
Stoke to Newcastle only:	7.30am 10.05am 11.25am 1.30pm 3.25pm 4.30pm
	5.35pm 7.50pm and 9.18pm
Stoke to Silverdale:	8.15am (Sundays at 1.20pm)

	UP
Market Drayton to Stoke:	10.30am 3.15pm 6.10pm and 8.20pm
	(Sundays at 9.55am and 8.15pm)
Newcastle to Stoke only:	7.40am 10.15am 12.00noon 2.15pm 3.35pm
	5.05pm 5.45pm 8.15pm and 9.30pm
Silverdale to Stoke:	8.50 (Sundays at 1.40pm)

A fortnight after the opening, the *Staffordshire Times* remarked that the passenger traffic on the new line had been 'very satisfactory, considering so little notice had been given' and continued 'we have no doubt, when travellers beyond Market Drayton understand the route, this branch will be very extensively patronised and will not only bring a good deal of traffic to the North Stafford company but will also greatly

benefit the district and towns which it passes.' Despite these express-
ions of confidence and allowing for the generous definition of the word
'towns', the long-term effect upon the rural inhabitants — who had
managed well enough hitherto — cannot have been outstanding. For
the next sixty years or so, cattle would continue to be driven on the
hoof from Drayton smithfield to places several miles away, and
country folk had long been accustomed to trudging considerable
distances with a market basket on each arm; nevertheless, a fair
amount of agricultural produce — notably milk — was at once
attracted to the new railway and, indeed, farmers were soon to realise
that more profit could be made from sending milk to London and other
large centres than by selling it locally!

Certain correspondents to the *Sentinel* were rather less than enthusiastic. On 5 March (1870) a Burslem resident bemoaned the fact that
he could not reach Stoke in time for the only train that would enable
him to travel to Shrewsbury and back on the same day. On 2 April, a
Silverdale gentleman drew attention to the 'miserable' accommodation provided by the railway company at that place, saying: '. . . the
new station is out of the way and the fares were raised — on the
principle, I suppose, of making people pay more for increased incon-
venience. The Silverdale passenger traffic has fallen off, I am told,
about 400 passengers a week since the Market Drayton line was
opened . . . 'tis a pity the railway company is so rich that it can do
without the patronage of Silverdale residents.' This was a reference to
the new station, which had been built on the outskirts of the village,
some 300yds to the west of the original (1863) terminus near the
church, and it seems that the complaint was well-founded for on 26
May the *Sentinel* reported: 'We hear the North Staffordshire Railway
Company contemplate providing a small station to be erected near the
centre of Church Street (opposite the junction of Crown Street)
specially for the convenience of passengers Newcastle-wards. The
present station is capacious and well fitted up, but — as proved by the
greatly diminished traffic since its opening — it is too far from the
village to be of service to those who desire to travel to Newcastle or
Stoke. Doubtless the accommodation station will be the means of
restoring the Silverdale passenger traffic.' (This 'accommodation station', consisting of two short platforms and a wooden shelter, was
taken into use in July 1871 and remained in service as 'Crown Street
halt' until June 1949.)

Another correspondent urged the running of 'half holiday excursions to such health resorts as Norton-in-Hales, to which we are
obliged to fly for want of a public park in the Potteries'. Again, the
NSR were quick to adopt this suggestion and Norton-in-Hales soon
became a popular venue for country outings and Sunday School
'treats' and the village was featured as a minor tourist attraction in the

Stoke station, c 1893. 'Newcastle bay' with branch line stock on right and subway to Up platform in foreground. Photograph taken immediately after building of new overall roof and installation of electric lighting. (Manifold photograph in George Dow Collection).

Newcastle station, King Street frontage, in 1902 — decorated for the Coronation of King Edward VII. (Newcastle Museum)

Down train at Newcastle, c. 1895, headed by Class 'A' 2-4-0T, No. 35. The signalman is receiving the token for the single line through the tunnels. Note the covered ramp leading from the Up platform to King Street overbridge and the street level booking hall. (Newcastle Museum)

Class 'D' 0-6-0T No 152 at Newcastle Down platform, looking down from Station Walks. This engine was built at Stoke in 1898 and survived to become LMS No 1597, being scrapped in 1936. To the rear of the platform is a short bay and the curving single track into the goods yard, which followed the line of the old Junction Canal. The further course of the canal is marked by the spire of St Paul's Church, beyond which lay the original terminal basin in Stubbs Field. (Dr J.R. Hollick)

Newcastle station, looking west towards Brampton level crossing, c. 1905. The Down distant signal for the crossing box is bracketed with the platform starter. Leafy Station Walks to the right, and the approaching locomotive has just passed under Queen Street bridge. (G.N. Nowell-Gossling)

An aerial view of Knutton Forge, looking north, c. 1925. The Market Drayton branch runs across the centre of the photograph, with Knutton Forge Junction signal box to the left and Knutton halt just off picture to right. The Pool Dam branch curves round behind the chimneys towards its crossing over Silverdale Road (in foreground) along which the electric tramwire standards can just be discerned. (Author's collection)

Looking east from the colliery waste tip at Silverdale, c. 1950. The curvature of the Market Drayton branch to avoid the church and the long row of cottages (known as The Brighton and since demolished) is noticeable. The pre-1870 terminus of the branch was to the rear of the church, to the left of which the route of the original Audley line can be seen running off the centre of the picture. (E.J.D. Warrillow)

Burley Colliery (Apedale) c. 1900. Hereabouts was the northern terminus of Gresley's canal. Manning Wardle 0-6-0ST (No 222) Burley *in foreground, with dumb buffered Midland Coal Coke & Iron Company's wagons. (The late H. Minshull)*

Silverdale at *Silverdale, c. 1880. This locomotive (Manning Wardle No 169 of 1863) was withdrawn from haulage duties at the colliery in 1902 and adapted for use as a stationary winding engine, remaining at work until 1973. (Geoff Monks)*

Apedale Ironworks, c. 1900, showing unidentified Manning Wardle 0-6-OST with NSR brake van. (The late H. Minshull)

Three-span reinforced concrete bridge over the M6 motorway, looking towards Keele. The site of Keele Park station is behind the camera. The bridge has an overall length of 90 metres and was constructed in 1961. (Author's collection)

Rail motor No 2 at Silverdale Up platform, c. 1910. The 'Knotty' possessed three of these vehicles, all built by Beyer Peacock & Co Ltd of Manchester, with coachwork by the Preston Carriage & Wagon Co. Ltd (later Dick, Kerr). (Terry Mountford)

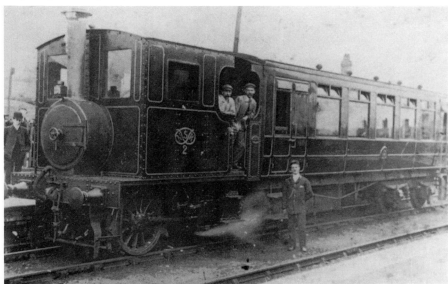

BR Class 08 0-6-0 shunter on inspection train, approaching Silverdale along the neglected Audley line — soon to be lifted. The signals relate to the parallel Market Drayton branch. (c. 1964) (M.J. Fell)

Madeley Chord signal box (1962-71). Up main line express in background. (M.J. Fell)

Silverdale station, looking west towards Keele in 1964. Note water tank at far end of Down platform and slopes of colliery waste tip on right (M.J. Fell)

The same scene in July 1976, photographed from the new footbridge and showing the hopper for loading 'merry-go-round' trains on the former Up line. The Down platform has been curtailed to enable the track to be slewed. (John & Jenny Williamson)

Madeley Chord lower level, looking south. The train on the Down fast line is passing under the branch line bridge. (M.J. Fell)

Madeley Road station (closed in 1931) looking towards Madeley Chord in May 1964. This was the only branch station with combined living quarters; the house was still occupied at the time of the photograph and the television aerial will be noted. The building was demolished in 1979. (M.J. Fell)

Pipe Gate station (Up side) c. 1910, before erection of separate porters' room at far end of station building. Note the floral display and the cinder-covered sleepers. (Lens of Sutton)

NSR Class 'A' 2-4-0T, No 35, heads an Up passenger train of 4-wheeled stock at Pipe Gate in 1895. This engine was built at Stoke in 1881, fitted with larger driving wheels in 1888 and converted to 2-4-2T in 1898 to carry an extended coal bunker. It became LMS No 1455 and was withdrawn from service in 1932. (L.&G.R.P. 23216)

Pipe Gate, looking east in 1934. The line of point rod supports between the Up and Down tracks is in preparation for the singling of the branch from Silverdale, when the entire signalling system was revised to LMS standards. The wagon loads of girders in front of the NSR warehouse (on left) are for the new creamery then being built off picture to right. Note the McKenzie & Holland ground disc. (Author's collection)

Pipe Gate station in 1966, ten years after cessation of the passenger service. The line converges to single track in the distance. (M.J. Fell)

Norton-in-Hales station in 1955. The site of the 16-lever signal box, which was purchased privately, can be judged by the opening under the one-time Down platform, through which passed the point rods and signal wires. (Author's collection)

Silverdale Junction in October 1966. Former GWR line to Nantwich to left, 'Knotty' branch to right. Note the 15 mph speed restriction for the branch. (M.J. Fell)

In the 'North Staffordshire' yard at Market Drayton, c. 1906. The serial number of the cattle truck is misleading as the Knotty owned fewer than 70 such vehicles at that time. (Salop County Library)

Market Drayton station from Adderley Road bridge, c. 1910. Cattle market in right distance and branch train of NSR coaches at left-hand ('bay') platform. (Lens of Sutton)

NSR No 164 at Market Drayton, c. 1921. This was the last of six 0-6-0 tender engines (Class '159') supplied by Nasmyth, Wilson & Co in 1900 — one or other of which handled the branch's freight traffic for many years. LMS Nos 2356/8678; withdrawn from service in 1934. (Author's collection)

Former NSR No 89 (Class 'New L', built at Stoke in 1913) poses in LMS days outside Drayton shed. This engine had previously spent some time in the London area, where its boiler mountings were reduced for working lines with limited overhead clearance. (Author's collection)

Fairburn 2-6-4T at the branch platform, Market Drayton, c. 1960. (Author's collection)

Pannier tank No 9636 takes water at Market Drayton before resuming its journey to Crewe. The starting signal is 'off' but the Silverdale Junction distant remains at danger. (Author's collection)

Southbound 'Pines Express' passing through Market Drayton in 1963. This through service from Manchester (London Road) to Bournemouth dated back to 1910; it was finally withdrawn in 1967. (Bernard Holland)

Market Drayton station in 1966, three years after all passenger working ceased. The footbridge has lost its roof and the atmosphere is generally forlorn. (Author's collection)

Knotty's advertisements — on a par with Rudyard Lake and Alton Towers.

Little more than a year after the opening of the branch, the NSR found it expedient to adjust the passenger timetable, thus producing a fresh spate of protest. A letter to the *Staffordshire Advertiser* read: '. . . practically all serviceable communication with the South by the new line to Market Drayton has ceased to exist, no passenger train reaching Wellington before 2 o'clock. (This) timetable is so cunningly devised that it is difficult to believe that the ingenious compiler is not instigated by some special grievance against our Borough!'

A second correspondent described as 'perfectly absurd' the fact that there was now no train from Stoke to beyond Newcastle until after 10.00am and that the train which formerly left Market Drayton at 10.30, in time to catch the connections from Stoke to Derby and Macclesfield had been withdrawn.

In June 1871 the North Staffordshire Naturalists' Field Club, whose members then — and for many years afterwards — frequently made use of the railways for their excursions, were obliged to make a nine miles drive from Market Drayton to Hawkestone Park instead of a one mile journey from Hodnet (W & DR) station as there was no onward connection from Drayton until 1.35pm. The Club's secretary commented upon this 'very awkward arrangement for Potteries people who go into Shropshire' but rejoiced that on this occasion the day was fine ('one of few in this watery summer') and the enforced drive was enjoyed by all concerned.

CHAPTER 5

THE FRUITFUL YEARS: 1870-1914

The original passenger station at Market Drayton was enlarged following the arrival of the Knotty and a single road engine shed was erected by the NSR adjacent to the new cattle market sidings (known as the North Staffordshire yard). In about 1880 the shed was extended to house the two branch locomotives (one passenger, one goods) that were stabled at Market Drayton for many years; the associated turntable was the property of the GWR. By a joint agreement dated 31 December 1877, the working and maintenance of Silverdale Junction was financed by the NSR, but the staff and signalling equipment were wholly Great Western. The main station building (on the town side) was of the GWR's 'French Renaissance' style, with ornamental iron-work to embellish the roof line and two square-topped pavilions at either end. Under the terms of the 1877 agreement, the NSR handed over the precise sum of £4,141 8s 8d — which had been assessed as their share of the station's cost and running expenses since the opening of the line from Silverdale — and in return the GWR undertook to afford the Knotty full and equal facilities 'as if it were its own traffic'.

The W & DR was embodied in the Great Western in 1866, but although worked by the major company, the N & MDR retained a nominal independence until 1897 when it, too, was absorbed. The through route provided the GWR with a tenuous hold on Crewe (where a two-road engine shed was installed at Gresty Lane) but the dream of a direct line to Manchester never materialised and there is a persistent, though apparently unfounded, rumour that the spacious Queen's Park — which was given to the townspeople of Crewe by the LNWR, ostensibly to mark the 1887 Jubilee — was sited so as to thwart the GWR's onward advance. In later years through carriages were operated via Market Drayton to places south of Wellington — and after 1910 the Manchester portion of the GWR/LSWR joint service to Bournemouth — but the link never fulfilled its promise as an effective passenger route to and from Manchester and a retired district superin-tendent of the GWR, writing in the *Railway Magazine* in 1930, estimated his company's share of the traffic at London Road and Exchange stations to have been 'an optimistic one per cent'. The line remained something of a backwater and was the very last section of the GWR to be equipped with the block telegraph — in 1891.

In November 1870 a small wayside station was opened between Keele and Pipe Gate. It was known as Madeley, then Madeley Manor for a few months only during 1871 and thereafter Madeley Road for the remaining sixty years of its active(?) existence. The site — close by the overgrown ruins of the Offley family's Tudor manor house — was quite isolated and as the centre of Madeley was some two miles distant, the volume of traffic did not call for any staff other than the officer in charge. There were no points or sidings and a four-lever ground frame on the down platform operated home and distant signals as required. The signals were normally kept at the 'all clear' position and certain trains did not stop unless signalled to do so. The branch's important 'London train' (Market Drayton depart 12.22pm; Euston arrive 4.05pm) was scheduled to halt only 'on notice being given to the guard at Pipe Gate'. In common with other stations on the branch, some milk traffic was handled and a purpose-built slide was used to convey full (17 gallons) churns to the up platform from the road bridge above. It was the first station on the branch to be closed (in July 1931) but the combined living quarters continued to be occupied for the next thirty years or so.

Construction of the 7½ miles long Audley line was beset by unforeseen difficulties. Not only were 'the cuttings' proving increasingly troublesome, but also the connections to the numerous sub-standard colliery sidings en route, and although mineral trains began to run from July 1870 onwards, a further ten years would elapse before the permanent way and signalling installation finally satisfied the Board of Trade's requirements for the safety of passenger traffic. At the company's half-yearly meeting in August 1880 — several weeks after the line had at long last been fully commissioned — the chairman referred to the considerable expense that had been incurred and reported that no less than £12,000 had been spent on the junction with the Harecastle-Crewe main line at Alsager, 'so as to prevent any possible chance of accident to the main line trains(!) Priority having thus been established, he went on to explain that 'the great competition going on between the Midland and the North Western obliges us to run fast trains between Crewe and Derby and it is absolutely necessary from every economical point of view that the junction should be perfectly secure'. To avoid the 'cuttings' more and more traffic for the Audley branch was being routed via Honeywall, but this necessitated a reversal at the latter place and — not without some opposition by local mine owners (because of the additional mileage charges) — the NSR prepared a bill for the laying of a short eastwards-facing spur between Keele station and Honeywall to provide for through running to and from the Market Drayton line. The enabling Act was obtained on 26 August 1880 and the new spur was taken into use in October 1881, upon which the tracks were lifted from the western curve and the Honeywall signal box was dismantled. A replacement box (Keele Junction) was erected in the fork of the revised lay-out just west of the bridge over the Newcastle to Madeley road.

On 26 June 1880 the *Staffordshire Advertiser* had reported that the Government Inspector had 'gone over and approved of the line from Keele to Harecastle (sic) (and) it will be opened for passenger traffic on Monday (28 June).' Four trains would run each weekday, calling at the new stations of Leycett, Halmerend and Audley; on Sundays there would be two trains each way. The newspaper believed that the line would prove to be 'of great convenience to the inhabitants of the Audley district' and on 3 July recorded: 'The new line was opened for passenger traffic on Monday morning. The first train was well laden with passengers anxious to have the privilege of riding upon the railway for the first time and during the week the railway has been the principal point of interest to the inhabitants of the district through which it passes. The young people have been particularly good customers of the company'.

Three days prior to the opening a special trip was organised for members of the Audley Board of Guardians, culminating in a luncheon at the railway company's North Stafford Hotel at Stoke. There were the inevitable toasts and the chairman for the day, Mr Rigby (a prominent local colliery owner) expressed his belief that 'it would prove a fair district to work and the railway would receive increasing support.' The station buildings on the branch were described as 'neat and convenient structures' and though built of wood for cheapness, there can be no doubt as to their durability as they remained intact for many years after their original purpose was only a memory. On 1 July 1889 a fourth station was opened close to the junction with the main line to Crewe; at first called 'Talke & Alsager Road', the name was simplified to 'Alsager Road' in May 1902. Water cranes were provided here for the use of the branch locomotives.

The country on either side of the Market Drayton branch was visited regularly by the North Staffordshire Hunt, whose kennels had been established at Trentham in 1862 and the railway company provided special facilities in the way of horse boxes and first-class carriages to the station most convenient to the meeting. The Woore district (Pipe Gate station) was — and still is — a popular venue and the Hunt's first historian (C J Blagg), writing in 1902, commented '. . . those members who live on the Draycott and Dilhorne side . . . can only hunt at Woore by using the North Staffordshire Railway as their covert hack'.

Pipe Gate soon became a busy rail-head for the surrounding area, with a substantial trade in timber and cattle; the 1878-1900 Ordnance Survey maps show a small cattle market adjacent to the Chetwode Arms Inn. A firm of coal merchants, James Meakin & Sons, who owned a small fleet of railway wagons, established their main office in the station goods yard, operating branch depots at Norton-in-Hales, Market Drayton and Audlem. In 1883 Henry Edwards & Son, of

London, built a creamery and milk condensing plant at Pipe Gate and later acquired the premises of the former Britannia iron foundry in Stafford Street, Market Drayton, now occupied by the Creamery garage. For many years large quantities of milk were despatched daily along the branch and by the mid-1920s this traffic had grown to such an extent as to require a special working to London. A locomotive ran down from Stoke each evening and around 1929-31 some of the few surviving ex-LNWR 'Jumbo' 2-4-0s were thus employed, notably the venerable *Snowdon* (LNWR No 2191, LMS Nos 5001 and 25001) which was to be the last of its class in regular service. Other visiting Jumbos included *Director, Princess Beatrice* and *John Ramsbottom*, the last-named in unaccustomed LMS crimson livery. These engines were based at Rugby and were rostered to act as pilot to the 4.0pm ex-Euston to Manchester train as far as Stoke, where they were usually turned before proceeding down the branch tender first; sometimes, however, the turntable at Market Drayton would be utilised, according to traffic requirements. Referring to this working, a correspondent to the *Railway Magazine* in October 1930 quoted an occasion when the train engine (No 5967 *L/Cpl J A Christie, V.C.* of the 'Claughton' class) failed at Rugeley and was detached by the pilot (*Snowdon*) which then took over the heavily laden seven-coach train — not bad for a 50 years old veteran! In 1935 a much larger creamery was built on the south side of Pipe Gate station, with direct rail access, and the simultaneous introduction of glass-lined tank wagons enabled the former pick-up arrangements by normal passenger train to be resumed. Since World War II the entire system of rural milk collection has undergone a radical change and in the mid-1960s the premises (latterly owned by Express Dairies) were taken over by the Phoenix Rubber Company, of Slough, for the manufacture of plastics.

In 1885 a permanently equipped race course was laid out on farm land about half a mile north of Pipe Gate station and annual meetings were held there until 1963, when the buildings were purchased for the North Staffordshire Hunt committee to avoid future competition with their own point-to-point races at Mucklestone. From the outset special race trains were run to Pipe Gate from a number of Midlands towns, such as Birmingham, and additional staff were brought in to deal with the crowds — often exceeding 8,000 people. As both the Up and Down platforms had a siding alongside, all occupying rolling stock was cleared in advance of race days to provide extra accommodation for the visiting trains, the displaced wagons being stored in the little-used yard at Norton-in-Hales and at Keele.

Also in 1885 the Silverdale mines and ironworks were leased to the Butterley Company of Alfreton, Derbyshire, but the furnaces were already past their prime and production had ceased by 1902, when Butterley decided not to renew the lease. For a short while another

Ralph Sneyd (1863-1949), who had inherited the Keele estate some seven years previously, seems to have attempted to revive a direct family interest in the works, but in 1903 mining operations were transferred to the newly-founded Silverdale Company. In the meantime, Sneyd indulged his passion for horse-racing by setting up training and breeding stables, in connection with which a horse loading dock was built at Keele station. A steeplechase course was created in the park and at Sneyd's request the NSR constructed a small station ('Keele Park') between Keele and Madeley Road, adjacent to the overbridge serving Stony Low farm. Signalling was operated from a ground frame and the station remained in occasional use from October 1896 to May 1907, when the buildings were dismantled and removed to Tean, on the Cheadle Railway, which the Knotty had taken over in January of that year. The race course lay almost one mile distant, to the south of the present-day motorway service area; its existence is commemorated by 'Racecourse Farm'. Owing to a deterioration in the family fortunes, racing at Keele was virtually at an end by 1901 and Sneyd had taken up residence in the south of England, having leased the hall to H.I.H. the Grand Duke Michael of Russia — who had been exiled for contracting a morganatic marriage. The Grand Duke remained at Keele for about ten years, during which time he took an active part in local affairs and was elected high steward of Newcastle. These great days were long remembered by the villagers, in particular a visit in July 1903 by King Edward VII, who travelled from Euston to Whitmore and back by a special train drawn by the Webb four-

[1892] **STOKE, SILVERDALE, & MARKET DRAYTON.—N S** (16-17)

cylinder compound engine which bore the royal name. The rather mean station at Keele was never used on such occasions and distinguished guests at the hall were conveyed by road from the main line stations at Whitmore or Stoke. Ralph Sneyd was appointed Colonel of the Staffordshire Yeomanry in World War I but he never returned to live at Keele; he died in Wiltshire in December 1949, having sold the hall and part of the estate to the progenitors of the University College of North Staffordshire — now Keele University.

Sneyd's associate, Francis Stanier (who was a director of the NSR from 1865 until his death in 1900) was rated among the most successful ironmasters in North Staffordshire. Renowned for his public works and benefactions, he was three times mayor of Newcastle under Lyme and a one-time high sheriff of Shropshire. In the early 1870s he purchased some 7,000 acres of Shropshire countryside and took up residence at Peplow Hall, between Hodnet and Crudgington. He appears to have been instrumental in persuading the GWR to build a station to serve the hall (for there was little other property in the vicinity) and Peplow figures in the time tables from 1873 onwards. This enabled Stanier to travel by rail to Silverdale, from where he would be conveyed to the Apedale works in his private saloon (by way of the Grove mineral line) hauled by one of his company's locomotives. In 1890 the Apedale complex was formed into the Midland Coal, Coke & Iron Company, which for the next forty years or so was to provide the main source of employment for the surrounding areas of Chesterton and Knutton. One of the first acts of the new company was to complete a mineral line from the northern end of Apedale to the Minnie and Podmore pits of Craig & Sons at Halmerend, with connections to the Audley branch at Halmerend station. On 12 January 1918 the Minnie pit was to achieve lasting notoriety by staging the worst disaster in the history of the North Staffordshire coalfield, whereby 155 men and boys lost their lives.

The separate demands of the Silverdale and Apedale plants gave rise to a distinct pattern of mineral traffic over the contiguous sections of the Market Drayton branch and an intensive system of 'private' working over NSR metals developed. The lay-out of the respective rail links with the branch was designed to facilitate through movements (a) between Silverdale and the Pool Dam and Brook Lane wharves at Newcastle and (b) between Apedale and the Marsh wharf (Newcastle) and Stoke. In addition, inter-works traffic used the Drayton line between Apedale and Knutton Junctions — a practice dating back to the earliest days of the branch — and for many years a passenger service for employees was run from Newcastle to accommodate the various shifts. This train, familiarly known as the 'Apedale Paddy', consisted of a rake of ex-NSR four-wheeled carriages with a brake van and time table stops were made at Brampton and Liverpool Road halts

THE COALFIELD

SHOWING PRINCIPAL MINERAL
LINES ⊢ − ⊣ AND COLLIERIES. (▲)
STATIONS SHOWN. ●—

(after their opening in 1905) as well as at Apedale Junction and the
level crossing of Lower Milehouse Lane at Knutton Gate, though
there were no platforms at the two last-named places and the stops may
well have been unauthorised. In fact, unofficial stops seem to have
been the rule — so much so that the train would be almost empty when
it reached the Apedale terminus, the passengers having already alight-
ed to suit their individual needs. So-called 'Paddy' trains were operated in other districts and it may be inferred that a high proportion of
the workforce was of Irish extraction; there was an influx of Irish
immigrants to North Staffordshire during the famine-stricken 1840s.
Before the advent of mechanical road transport the outlying collieries
were very largely dependent upon the railway and the Knotty ran an

early morning service to Leycett. Here again, it was customary for the train to slow down some distance from the station, whereupon the miners would jump down and dash across the tracks to the colliery lamp room, where the maxim of 'first come, first served' always applied. In the days before pit head baths the condition of the Paddy trains — often lit only by candles supplied by the passengers — may be imagined. Recalling this period in a letter to the *Sentinel* (in March 1963) a former miner stated that the carriages were never cleaned and were blacker than the returning colliers themselves, hence — in a less fastidious age — the service was commonly known as the 'nigger train'.

The passing of the Light Railways Act in 1896 encouraged the Knotty to seek Orders for the running of regular passenger trains over the Apedale branch and a number of other mineral lines throughout the system, but the powers obtained (in 1906) were never exercised, for the impact of rival modes of transport was increasing. As early as 1861 a horse-drawn street railway had been installed between Burslem and Hanley, being converted to steam haulage and extended to Stoke and Longton some twenty years later. In 1898 the Potteries Electric Traction Company was launched and electric trams were soon operating on a wide scale, including a Newcastle-Silverdale service which ran parallel to the Market Drayton branch for much of its length. The trams and their successors the motor buses (the first of which appeared in the Potteries in 1904) had, by their use of the common highway, a natural advantage in catering for door-to-door customers and, like most other railways at that time, the Knotty soon encountered mounting competition. Early in 1905 the NSR's chairman announced a comparative loss of 175,000 passengers, which he attributed to 'poverty in the district, the lack of football matches and tramway competition' (in that order) but there can have been no doubt where lay the greatest threat, for that same year three 'rail motor cars' were purchased from Beyer Peacock & Company at a cost of £6,000, to cater especially for workmen; weekly tickets would be issued at fares, as low as sixpence (2½p) for twelve journeys. Rail car No 1 was placed in service on the Market Drayton branch in July (1905) and efforts were made to attract passengers back to the railway by introducing a number of lineside halts — at Hartshill & Basford (at the Stoke end of the Newcastle tunnels), Brampton (the turning point of the old Junction Canal), Liverpool Road and Knutton (adjacent to the ironworks). For a time cars ran through to Keele and Leycett (for the colliery), the first of the day reaching Leycett at 5.28am, but their initial success was progressively lost to the more flexible road vehicles and they ended their days on a shuttle service between Stoke and Newcastle. The three cars lay derelict at Crewe Works for a number of years following the national grouping of railway companies and all were broken up in 1927. Three of the purpose-built halts did not long survive the demise of the rail car service; Brampton was dismantled in 1923 and Hartshill & Basford and Knutton were closed three years later. Crown Street and Liverpool Road continued to be visited by certain passenger trains and provided a convenient means of transport for employees of the Enderley Mills clothing factory at Newcastle. Crown Street was finally closed in June 1949 and some time previously only one unadvertised workmen's train had called there; Liverpool Road lingered on until March 1964, when the last remaining passenger trains were withdrawn between Stoke and Silverdale.

From the outset, the Knotty had unrestricted use of Great Western metals between Silverdale Junction and Market Drayton station (a distance of sixteen chains) and onwards to Hodnet with passengers and cattle and to Wellington with freight. In 1899 a station was opened at Tern Hill, mid-way between Market Drayton and Hodnet and a cheese factory was erected alongside. As at Peplow, nearby dwellings were few and not all passenger trains were scheduled to stop. Latterly, however, this station enjoyed a period of comparative prosperity following the establishment of a large Royal Air Force camp in the neighbourhood just prior to World War II, which created an unwonted passenger demand and necessitated the laying of additional siding accommodation.

In October 1907 the *Railway Magazine* commented upon the current practice as follows: 'The most peculiar working of the North Staffordshire Railway's passenger trains to "foreign" lines is that of the one on Tuesdays only, over the Great Western Railway from Market Drayton to Hodnet, a distance of 5¾ miles. This train starts from Market Drayton at 11.55am, arrives at Hodnet at 12.04pm and returns empty at 12.10pm, arriving at 12.19pm. Tuesday is Hodnet market day and the running of this through train by the North Staffordshire Railway is an instance of the arrangements made by that enterprising railway to provide convenience for the public. If the train were not to run through, passengers for Hodnet market from the North Staffordshire Railway would have to wait at Market Drayton from 11.55am until the 1.46pm Great Western Railway train . . . Another NSR train runs through to Hodnet on Thursdays and Saturdays, leaving Market Drayton at 2.56pm and arriving at Hodnet at 3.05pm. This train also on both days returns empty, leaving Hodnet at 3.20pm.'

On its part, the Great Western was empowered to operate a daily goods train from Shrewsbury (depart 4.10am) via Wellington to Stoke, returning in mid-morning, and in 1903 the very generous timings for the sixteen-mile journey between Market Drayton and Stoke were: Market Drayton dep. 6.30am — arr. Stoke 8.00am; Stoke dep. 10.30am — arr. Market Drayton 12.15pm; this suggests that a pick-up service was allowed for, although within the writer's memory such occasions were extremely rare. This use of the Drayton branch lingered on into LMS days and did not cease until 1928; by that time the visiting locomotive was usually a Dean 0-6-0 tender engine and its unfamiliar green livery — with a brake van mysteriously labelled 'Oxley Sidings' — provided a great attraction for at least one small boy who lived near the line! This 'foreign' working was balanced by a NSR trip to Wellington and back, hauled for many years by one of the Knotty's six 0-6-0 tender engines of the '159' class which were supplied by Naysmith Wilson & Company in 1900. All six lasted well into the LMS era and No 159, the first of its class, was allocated to Market Drayton shed on delivery. In NSR days its shed mate would be one of the 2-4-0 and 2-4-2 tanks so widely used for branch passenger services on the Knotty and some of the Class 'A' engines, eight of which were built at Stoke between 1878 and 1881, were early 'regulars' — especially NSR No 35, the last but one of the batch. Later these were superseded by an improved version (Class 'B'), one of which (NSR No 48) was stabled at Market Drayton for a long period, survived to become LMS No 1446 and was not withdrawn from service until 1929.

Soon after the completion of the Trentham Park branch, in 1910, preparations were made to extend this line to meet the Pool Dam branch at Newcastle and to introduce a through passenger service to the Market Drayton branch at Knutton and beyond. From Trentham the proposed route ran up the valley of the River Trent to Hanford (where a station was planned) and thence followed the Newcastle (Lower) Canal to Brook Lane. An Order for the 'Trentham, Newcastle-under-Lyme & Silverdale Light Railway' was obtained in 1912 and with the promise of a £50,000 loan from the Staffordshire County Council, construction began at the southern end just prior to the outbreak of World War I. A substantial girder bridge was rolled across the main Newcastle to Stone road at Trentham in September 1914, but wartime conditions brought the works to a standstill and the scheme was finally abandoned on the formation of the LMS group in 1923. The bridge remained as a mute reminder of past aspirations until 1940, when it was dismantled for scrap metal during another World War. The 1914-18 War led to a reduction in passenger services generally and it was predictable that the Knotty would refuse a request for a station or halt to serve the hamlet of Onneley, mid-way between Madeley Road and Pipe Gate. This was in 1917 and while the wishes of local inhabitants were never fulfilled, a winding lane leading down to what is left of the Market Drayton branch still bears the epithet of 'Station Road'.

FROM 1910 BRADSHAW

STOKE, NEWCASTLE, HARECASTLE, and MARKET DRAYTON.—North Staffordshire.

Down. — Week Days.

Miles	Down.	mrn (Mondays only)	m	mrn (Weds. only)	mrn	mrn	mrn	aft	aft (Saturdays only)	aft (Saturdays only)	aft (Saturdays only)	aft	aft	aft (Mondays only)	aft (Except Saturdays)	aft (Mondays and Saturdays)	aft (Except Mons. & Sats.)	aft (Weds. only)	aft (Sats. only)	m (Except Mondays and Saturdays)	aft	aft (Saturdays only)
	Stoke dep.	7 17	7 33	9 3	9 20	11 5	1135	1255	1 30	2 15	2 26	3 58	4 55	6 50	7 38	8 0	8 0		8 45	9 5	9r5	1110
2	Newcastle	7 23	7 39	9 9	9 26	1111	1141	1 1	1 35	2 21	2 32	4 4	5 1	6 56	7 44	8 5	8 6		8 51	9 11	9r11	1115
4¾	Silverdale	7 29	7 45	9 16	9 33	1118	1148	1 8	1 41	2 28	2 39	4 11	5 8	7 2	7 50	8 11	8 13		8 57	9 18	9r18	1121
6	Keele	...	7 49	9 20	9 37	1122	1152	1 12		2 33	2 43	4 15	5 12	...	7 54	8 15	8 17		9 1	9 22	9r22	...
7½	Leycett		7 53		...	...	1157	...		...	2 47	4 20	...		...	8 20	8 22				9s27	
9	Halmerend		7 57		...	...	12 2	...		...	2 51	4 25	...		...	8 24		8 26			9s32	
10½	Audley		8 1		...	...	12 7	...		...	2 56	4 30	...		...	8 28		8 29			9s37	
13¼	Alsager Road		8 8		...	...	1215	...		...	3 4	4 38	...		...	8 36		...			9s45	
15¼	Harecastle* 530 to 534 ar		8 13		...	...	1219	...		...	3 9	4 43	...		...	8 42		...			9s50	
8¾	Madeley Road		...	9 27	Sig.	1129	...	1 18		2 40	...	...	5 18		8 0	...		...	9 7		...	
11⅓	Pipe Gate, for Woore		...	9 34	9 48	1136	...	1 24		2 47	...	...	5 25		8 7	...		...	9 14		...	
14	Norton-in-Hales		...	9 43	9 55	1143	...	1 30		2 54	...	...	5 32		8 14	...		...	9 20		...	
17¼	Market Drayton 103 arr.		...	9 50	10 1	1150	...	1 35		3 0	...	...	5 37		8 20	...		...	9 26		...	

Down. — Sundays.

Down.	mrn	mrn	aft	aft	aft	
Stoke dep.	8 57	11 5	2 30	7 45	8 38	...
Newcastle	9 3	1111	2 36	7 51	8 44	...
Silverdale	9 10	1118	2 42	7 58	8 51	...
Keele	9 14	1122	2 46	8 2	8 55	...
Leycett	...	1127	2 50	8 7	...	...
Halmerend	...	1132	2 54	8 12	...	...
Audley	...	1137	2 59	8 17	...	...
Alsager Road	...	1144	3 5	8 25	...	...
Harecastle	...	1149	3 10	8 30	...	...
Madeley Road	9 20	...	...	...	9 2	...
Pipe Gate, for Woore	9 27	...	...	...	9 9	...
Norton-in-Hales	9 33	...	...	...	9 16	...
Market Drayton 103 arr.	9 39	...	...	...	9 22	...

Up. — Week Days.

Miles	Up.	mrn (Mondays only)	mrn	mrn	mrn	aft	aft (Saturdays only)	aft	aft	aft (Saturdays only)	aft (Weds. only)	aft (Sats. only)	aft	aft (Mondays only)	aft	aft m (Weds. only)	(Except Mons. & Sats.)	aft (Mondays only)	aft m (Except Mons. and Sats.)	aft (Saturdays only)	aft (Saturdays only)			
	Market Drayton dep.		8 30	...	1027	1225		...	3 35	...	4 15	5 10	...		6 55			...		...		...	...	...
3¼	Norton-in-Hales		8 37	...	1033	1231		...	3 42	...	4 23	5 17	...		7 2			...		...		...	...	...
5¾	Pipe Gate, for Woore		8 44	...	1039	1237		...	3 49	...	4 30	5 24	...		7 12			...		...		...	...	...
8¾	Madeley Road		8 51	...	1045	Sig.		...	3q56	...	4 37	5 31	...		7 19			...		...		...	...	...
—	Mls Harecastle dep.		...	9 0	...	...		2 0	...	4 10			5 35		...			9 20		10 5		...	...	...
—	2 Alsager Road		...	9 5	...	...		2 5	...	4 15			5 40		...			9 25		1010		...	...	...
—	4¾ Audley		...	9 13	...	...		2 12	...	4 22			5 47		...	8 30		9 32		1017		...	...	...
—	6¼ Halmerend		...	9 19	...	...		2 17	...	4 27			5 52		...	8 33		9 37		1022		...	...	...
—	7¾ Leycett		...	9 25	...	...		2 22	...	4 32			5 57		...	...	8 40	9 42		1027		...	...	...
11¼	Keele (above)	...	8 58	9 30	1051	1249	...	2 26	4 3	4 37	4 45	5 38	6 2	...	7 26	...	8 45	9 47	9 47	1032	...	...	...	...
12¾	Silverdale 537	7 35	9 2	9 35	1055	1253	1 50	2 30	4 7	4 42	4 53	5 43	6 6	7 10	7 31	...	8 49	9 52	9 52	1037	1130	...	...	...
15¼	Newcastle	7 40	9 10	9 42	11 1	1259	1 57	2 37	4 14	4 52	5 4	5 52	6 13	7 17	7 38	...	8 56	10 0	10 0	1045	1135	...	...	...
17¼	Stoke 530 to 535 arr	7 46	9 16	9 48	11 6	1 4	2 2	2 42	4 20	4 57	5 10	5 58	6 19	7 22	7 43	...	9 1	10 5	10 5	1051	1140	...	...	...

Up. — Sundays.

Up.	mrn	aft	aft	aft		
Market Drayton dep.	9 52	...	7 25	...	...	...
Norton-in-Hales	10 1	...	7 33	...	...	...
Pipe Gate, for Woore	1011	...	7 41	...	...	...
Madeley Road	1019	...	7 49	...	...	...
Harecastle dep.	...	1 40	...	9 0	...	...
Alsager Road	...	1 45	...	9 5	...	...
Audley	...	1 52	...	9 12	...	...
Halmerend	...	1 57	...	9 17	...	...
Leycett	...	2 2	...	9 21	...	...
Keele (above)	1026	2 6	7 56	9 25	...	...
Silverdale 537	1030	2 10	8 1	9 29	...	...
Newcastle	1037	2 17	8 9	9 36	...	...
Stoke 530 to 535 arr	1042	2 22	8 15	9 42	...	...

m Motor Car, one class only. q Does not call on Wednesdays except to take up for the Audley Branch. r Mondays and Saturdays. s Saturdays only. * Station for Kidsgrove.

☞ For **LOCAL TRAINS** between Stoke and Newcastle, see page 528.

STOKE and NEWCASTLE.—North Staffordshire.

Down. — Week Days.

Miles	Down.	m	mrn	m	mrn	m	mrn	mrn	mrn	mrn	mrn	mrn	mrn	mrn	mrn	m	aft	Sats. m	Sats. aft	Sats. m	Sats. aft	Sats. aft
	Stoke ¶ dep.	4 55	5 30	6 20	7 17	7 33	7 53	8 15	8 51	9y3	9 20	9 50	1018	11 5	1135	1150	12e27	1231	1255	1e13	1 30	2 15
2	Newcastle arr.	5 2	5 35	6 25	7 23	7 39	7 58	8 21	8 56	9y9	9 26	9 55	1023	1111	1141	1155	12e32	1236	1 1	1e20	1 35	2 21

Down.	aft	aft	aft	aft	aft	aft	aft	m	aft	aft	m	aft	aft	Sats. aft	Sats. m	Sats. aft	Sats. aft	Sats. aft				
Stoke ¶ dep.	2 26	3 25	3 58	4 33	4 55	5 12	5 40	6 20	6 50	7 38	8a0	8x0	8 33	8 45	9a5	9x5	9 50	1110	...	...	...	...
Newcastle arr.	2 32	3 30	4 4	4 38	5 1	5 17	5 45	6 25	6 56	7 44	8a6	8x5	8 38	8 51	9a11	9x11	9 55	1115	...	...	...	...

Down. — Sundays.

Down.	mrn	mrn	aft	aft	aft	aft
Stoke ¶ dep.	8 57	11 5	2 30	4 50	7 45	8 38
Newcastle arr.	9 3	11 11	2 36	4 55	7 51	8 44

Up. — Week Days.

Miles	Up.	mrn	m	m	mrn	mrn	mrn	mrn	mrn	mrn	mrn	mrn	mrn	m	c	aft	Sats. m	Sats. aft	Sats. aft	Sats. aft	Sats. m	Sats. aft	Sats. aft
	Newcastle ¶ dep.	5 40	6 30	6 50	7 40	8 10	8 30	9 3	9 10	9 42	10 0	1030	11 1	12 0	12 38	1259	1 15	1 57	2 37	2e50	3e20	3 50	4 14
2	Stoke 529-37 arr.	5 45	6 36	6 55	7 46	8 15	8 35	9 8	9 16	9 48	10 5	1035	11 6	12 5	12 43	1 4	1 21	2 2	2 42	2e55	3e25	3 56	4 20

Up.	aft	aft	aft	aft	aft	m	aft	aft	aft	aft	m	aft	aft	Sats. aft	Sats. aft	Sats. aft			
Newcastle ¶ dep.	4 52	5y4	5 22	5 52	6 13	7 0	7 17	7 38	8 10	8 43	8a56	10 0	10e30	10 45	11e20	11 35	...	...	...
Stoke 529 to 537 arr.	4 57	5y10	5 27	5 58	6 19	7 5	7 22	7 43	8 15	8 48	9a1	10 5	10e35	10 51	11e25	11 40	...	...	...

Up. — Sundays.

Up.	mrn	mrn	aft	aft	aft	aft
Newcastle ¶ dep.	8 45	10 37	2 17	5 0	8 9	9 36
Stoke 529 to 537 arr.	8 51	10 42	2 22	5 7	8 15	9 42

a Except Mondays and Saturdays. c Runs 6 minutes *earlier* on Saturdays. e Except Saturdays. m Motor Car, one class only. x Mondays and Saturdays. y Wednesdays only. ¶ "Halt" at Hartshill and Basford.

LEYCETT, SILVERDALE, STOKE, TRENTHAM, and STONE (Motor Cars—One class only).—North Staffordshire.

Up. — Week Days.

Miles	Up.	mrn	mrn	mrn	1,2,3	mrn	mrn	non	aft (Saturdays only)	aft	aft (Except Fris. and Sats.)	aft	aft (Fridays only)	aft	aft	aft	aft (Except Mons. and Sats.)	aft (Except Mons. and Sats.)
	Leycett dep.	5 45	...	...	9 25	...	...	...	1255	...	2 45	...	3 0	...	...	...	8 40	...
1	Keele	5 49	...	...	9 30	...	...	...	1 0	...	2 50	...	3 5	...	...	6 45	8 45	9 47
2½	Silverdale ¶	5 53	...	...	9 35	...	...	...	1 4	...	2 54	...	3 9	...	...	6 50	8 49	9 52
5	Newcastle ¶	6 4	6 50	...	10 0	...	...	12 0	1 15	...	3 8	...	3 23	...	...	7 0	8 56	10 0
7	Stoke ¶ 528 to 535	...	7 23	...	10 8	...	...	12 6	1 21	1 26	...	...	...	4 39	...	7 10	9 1	10 5
10	Trentham ¶ 532	...	7 30	8 10	1015	1115	1150	1218	...	1 37	...	2 47	...	4 50	5 22	7 17	...	...
—	Trentham Park arr.	...	7 35	8 15	1020	1120	1155	...	...	1 42	...	2 52	...	4 55	5 27	7 22	...	...
12	Barlaston (Tittensor)	...	...	...	...	...	...	1223e		...	...	...	...	...	...	...	...	...
14	Stone Junction arr.	...	...	...	...	...	...	1228e		...	...	...	...	...	...	...	...	...

Down. — Week Days.

Mls	Down.	mrn	mrn	mrn	mrn	1,2,3	mrn	aft (Saturdays only)	aft (Sats. only)	aft (Except Sats.)	aft (Except Saturdays)	aft	aft	aft	aft	aft	aft (Except Mons. and Sats.)	aft (Except Mons. and Sats.)	
—	Stone Junction dep.	...	...	...	...	...	...	...	...	1235	...	...	...	...	...	...	...	...	...
2	Barlaston (Tittensor)	...	...	...	...	...	...	...	...	1240	...	...	...	...	...	...	...	...	...
—	Trentham Park ¶ dep.	...	...	7 48	8 28	1035	1135	...	1238	...	1250	1 55	3 15	5 3	6 5	7 45	...	...	...
4	Trentham ¶	...	...	7 53	8 33	1040	1140	1219	1245	1245	1255	2 0	3 20	5 8	6 10	7 50	...	...	...
7	Stoke ¶ 528 to 535	4 55	7 33	...	8 43	1046	...	1231	1254	1254	1 13	...	3 27	...	6 20	7 56	8 0	9 5	...
9	Newcastle ¶	5 2	7 39	...	...	...	...	1236			1 20	...	...	...	6 25	...	8 6	9 11	...
11½	Silverdale 529	5 17	7 45	...	...	...	...	1246			1 33	...	...	...	6 34	...	8 13	9 18	...
13	Keele	5 22	7 49	...	...	...	...	1250			1 37	...	...	...	6 38	...	8 17	9 22	...
14	Leycett 529 arr.	5 28	7 53	...	...	...	...	1254			1 41	...	...	...	...	...	8 22	...	...

NOTES.

e Except Saturdays.

¶ "**Halts**" at Silverdale (Crown Street), Knutton, Newcastle (Liverpool Road and Brampton), between Silverdale Station and Newcastle Station; Hartshill and Basford, between Newcastle and Stoke; Whieldon Road, Mount Pleasant, and Sideway, between Stoke and Trentham; and Hanford Road, between Trentham and Trentham Park.

CHAPTER 6

CHANGES AND CLOSURES: 1914-1976

For several reasons World War I marked a turning point in the history of all railways and wartime government control presaged the formation of four major companies with effect from 1 January 1923. Post-war unrest seriously affected the industrial front and there was a general railway strike in the autumn of 1919, but the Knotty survived to become a constituent of the London Midland & Scottish Railway. The final (144th) annual general meeting of the NSR was an emotional affair, the chairman, Lord Anslow, referring to the 'deplorable loss' of the 'dear old Company', but in fact there was little apparent change on the branch lines for some years to come. As evidenced at Market Drayton, the Great Western retained its title and its marked individuality until well after nationalisation in 1948; eventually both the former GWR and NSR (LMS) lines became part of the Stoke Division of the London Midland Region of British Rail.

In the closing years of its independent existence the Knotty had designed a scheme for the extensive re-modelling of Stoke station, incorporating an avoiding freight loop from Etruria that would have pierced the Hartshill—Basford ridge and passed under the Market Drayton branch to the east of the Newcastle tunnels. An area to the south of the branch was to have been converted into Up and Down marshalling yards to enable the existing goods yard to be absorbed into an enlarged passenger station at Stoke. This bold plan was held in suspense by the impending amalgamation and the LMS found no need for it in the light of increasing competition by private road haulage. Stoke station itself still retains its original form of two long platforms; until 1966 there were Up and Down through roads between the platform lines, but in that year the Down road was removed to make room for catenary supports as the electrification programme advanced. Stoke rarely acted as a terminus, even for local services and thus, for example, a Rushton-Leek-Stoke passenger train would take up a working to Market Drayton or along the Audley branch within a few minutes of its arrival. There was, however, one additional road at the western end of the Down platform, usually referred to as the 'Newcastle bay' and it was from here that passenger trains originating at Stoke departed for Newcastle and stations beyond.

Soon after the grouping, the NSR bridge over the West Coast main line near Madeley Road was replaced by a steel girder structure which remains in use today, although reduced to a single track span. The nearby spur between the two railways remained trackless and in those early days of civil aviation the place name MADELEY was displayed on the embankment for the guidance of pilots, who regularly made use of the West Coast route for navigational purposes.

The year 1926 witnessed another and greater general strike (May 3-12), but its effect on the former Knotty lines was not so serious as elsewhere; volunteer strike breakers were 'plentiful' and 'small numbers of men returned to work daily'. On the final day of the strike, no fewer than 113 trains were operated from Stoke. The end of the decade coincided with widespread trade depression, bringing with it the catastrophic collapse of the Midland Coal, Coke & Iron Company's Apedale empire. Knutton forge was closed in 1929 but its three tall chimney stacks (known locally as 'Faith', 'Hope' and 'Charity') survived for another twenty years — despite some concern that they might act as a landmark for enemy aircrews during World War II. More than most, the Audley line depended upon the prosperity of the surrounding coalfield and the withdrawal of all passenger services (never its strong suit) in April 1931 evoked little surprise. That same year Madeley Road Station was closed, as well as the engine shed at Market Drayton.

The single-tracked Newcastle tunnels had been troublesome for many years — at least since 1913, when both GWR and GCR rolling stock was damaged through inadequate clearance — and by 1930 earth movements had affected the tunnel lining so seriously as to necessitate complete closure for repairs, passengers being conveyed by bus between Newcastle and Stoke stations. Mr G N Nowell-Gossling, whose father supervised the works, recalls that the longer tunnel (577yds) was re-lined with steel sections formerly in use on the London underground railway. Even so, conditions for engine crews were not greatly improved and owing to poor ventilation it was not unknown for a driver or fireman to be overcome by the fume-laden atmosphere — for this reason 'double heading' was forbidden. The final years, however, are said to have brought some consolation to local signalmen, who discovered that their telephones carried radio programmes induced from cables laid through the tunnels by a commercial broadcast company!

As the 1920s progressed, motor buses made increasing inroads into the rural catchment areas which hitherto had been almost wholly dependent upon the railway; in the towns, also, the electric trams succumbed in time and the entire system was abandoned in 1928, being replaced by the Potteries Motor Traction Company (PMT). To the south of the Market Drayton branch the PMT developed a frequent service between Newcastle and the Shropshire town, from where onward connections to Shrewsbury were provided by the Midland Red omnibuses. To the north, the Crosville Motor Company commenced daily workings from Knighton, through Woore, to Madeley and Newcastle and the same company's Newcastle-Whitchurch and New-castle-Chester services also ran via Keele and Madeley. In the early 1930s the PMT began a Saturday service to Newcastle (via Whitmore) which started from Pipe Gate station itself! To counter this competi-tion, the LMS introduced additional trains on market days and Satur-days — with little success — and for many years the basic timetable consisted of five down and four up trains, the Up mid-day ('London') train combining the coaching stock of the two morning Down trains. At the turn of the century there had been seven Down and six Up trains, plus one early morning working from Stoke to Pipe Gate and back, the timings of which were: Stoke dep. 6.35am, Pipe Gate arr. 7.05am; Pipe Gate dep. 7.15am, Stoke arr. 7.47am. One may wonder how many through passengers availed themselves of this facility, even in those motor-less days! After the 1923 grouping former NSR locomo-tives continued to work the branch, notably old No 89 (LMS No 2258), an 0-6-2 tank built at Stoke in 1913, which returned to Drayton shed in 1927 after a sojourn in the London area, where its boiler mountings were cut down for working on lines with limited clearance. By the outbreak of World War II all the ex-NSR engines had been withdrawn or sold and the ubiquitous Stanier tanks and Fowler six-coupled goods had taken over. The earliest four-wheeled coaching stock on the branch was replaced only gradually by more up-to-date six-wheelers, many of which were still running in LMS days. From the mid-1890s electricity began to supersede oil for carriage lighting — gas never being employed by the Knotty for this purpose — and in the 1930s some of the old company's side-corridor bogie coaches made occasion-al appearances. Latterly, three-coach sets of LMS metal-bodied stock predominated and the six years of British Rail's tenure brought little change to the branch.

On the Wellington-Nantwich line the 1930s saw the introduction of no fewer than seven intermediate unstaffed halts, in keeping with the Great Western's attempt to win back passengers, but railways general-ly were fighting a losing battle in this field and economies were called for. In 1933 work began on the reduction of the Silverdale-Market Drayton and Keele-Alsager Junction sections to single track. The junction at Keele was lifted and henceforward the two single lines ran side by side through Keele station and the tunnel into Silverdale station; this duplicated Up and Down working was recognised as a potential source of danger to permanent-way men and notices advising "particular care" were displayed at both entrances to the tunnel. Singling was completed as far as Pipe Gate (which was retained as a crossing point with two long storage sidings) by the autumn of 1934 and the remaining section followed, Norton-in-Hales ceasing to be a block post. The revised arrangements included the replacement of the

Knotty's graceful McKenzie & Holland semaphore signals by LMS upper quadrant versions and also supplanted were the rather charming ground (shunting) discs, which revolved on a vertical axis in proportion to the tension of the controlling wire!

World War II brought about the removal of station name boards (to confuse enemy parachutists!) and the blacking-out of trains and buildings. At Apedale Junction a long siding was trailed in to the Up line to serve a wartime armaments factory and workpeople's trains were run daily from Silverdale to the Royal Ordnance Depot at Swynnerton (near Stone), the coaching stock being stored overnight on the Audley line, in Silverdale tunnel. North Staffordshire escaped the brunt of aerial attack, and with the cessation of hostilities, nationaliation became the order of the day. The old railway companies were merged into regions of the newly appointed Railway Executive on and from 1 January 1948, but — as had been the case with the 1923 grouping — the lines serving Market Drayton were affected only gradually. One noticeable result of nationalisation, both of the railways and the mining industry, was the disappearance of the privately-owned wagon, which had made such a varied contribution to the pre-War goods train and for a time large numbers of these wagons were stored in the sidings at Pipe Gate, awaiting disposal.

It became increasingly clear, however, that the country railway station had had its day and it was scarcely surprising when, early in 1956, British Rail published their intention to withdraw the passenger service between Silverdale and Market Drayton — which by this time consisted of three trains each way on weekdays, all Sunday workings having already ceased. Following this announcement, despairing representations were made to the Transport Users' Consultative Committee, pointing out that the neighbourhoods of Pipe Gate and Norton-in-Hales would be deprived of public transport save for a skeleton bus service on Wednesdays and Saturdays. In reply it was stated that there was overwhelming evidence that for several years increasing use had been made of private vehicles and a recent census had shown that the average number of passengers booked over the branch from Market Drayton was nine by the morning train, twelve at mid-day and three in the evening, traffic in the reverse direction being of the same order. First class passengers had long been a rarity on the branch and the writer recalls that for many years only one gentleman had made regular use of this comparative luxury. Diesel mutliple units did not arrive in the district until 1956 and never had the opportunity to recover the situation, but in any case the distance of all the branch stations from centres of population or major shopping facilities was a vital factor at a period when most families had ready access to private transport. Inevitably, it was ordered that passenger services were to cease as from Monday 7 May 1956 and from the same date freight services would be terminated at Keele and Norton-in-Hales stations, though Pipe Gate would remain open for freight traffic and enquiries; parcels deliveries in the area served by the branch were to be made by road vehicle from Stoke-on-Trent.

There being no Sunday working, the last through passenger train was the 7.00pm from Market Drayton on Saturday 5 May, which carried its heaviest load for many a day — including a party of 40 pupils of the Knutton Secondary Modern School led by an enthusiastic teacher. The rake of four coaches was hauled by 2-6-4 tank No 42671 and its departure from the 'North Staffordshire bay' (actually the northern face of the Down island platform) was marked by exploding detonators. Small groups of mourners gathered at the five intermediate stations to witness the passing, but with a regrettable lack of feeling for such an historic occasion, the train's arrival at Stoke's No 1 platform went unheralded and minutes later its onward progress was coldly announced as 'the 7.55 for Birmingham New Street, calling at all stations'. So ended an era!

The Audley line was closed completely in January 1963 and for some time previously traffic had been virtually non-existent, its last mainstay, Leycett Colliery, having been shut down in 1957. The spur to Bignall Hill Colliery was closed at the same time and the link with Jamage Colliery had been broken in December 1947. The sole remaining passenger service — between Silverdale and Stoke — ceased to operate in March 1964, following a public inquiry at which protests were voiced by the Newcastle Borough Council and the National Society of Pottery Workers, the latter body being concerned that employees of the Wedgwood factory at Barlaston would no longer be able to travel by train from Silverdale to Wedgwood halt, which had been provided by the LMS in 1940 to serve the new works. The Borough Council's objection was that the proposed alternative bus service was inadequate and would not connect with main line trains at Stoke. These protests proved to be in vain and, the pottery workers having been assured that factory buses would be extended from Newcastle to Silverdale, all passenger trains were withdrawn on 2 March. As with the previous closure, the estimated saving was reported to be in the region of £5,000 per year.

On 9 September 1963 Market Drayton had lost its surviving passenger service to Wellington and Crewe, the Commissioners having claimed that a minimum annual saving of £50,000 would be effected thereby — the loss of passenger revenue was estimated at just under £10,000 a year. Meanwhile, however, an unprecedented amount of freight was passing between the former GWR system and the Market Drayton branch, reaching a peak of more than 10,000 tons weekly during 1962-3. This was largely owing to the progressive electrification of lines south of Stafford and through Stoke and to assist the movement of the re-routed traffic, tracks were laid along the spur connecting the former NSR and LNWR lines to the east of Madeley Road — for the first time since the embankment was formed almost 100 years before! Access was thus obtained to the Down slow line of the West Coast main route and to control operations an electro-mechanical signal box, named 'Madeley Chord' (from the geometry of the track lay-out), was erected on the south side of the Drayton branch, just west of the bridge over the main line. These developments were in accordance with a current plan to re-vitalise the entire line from Wellington, where a new double junction with the Shrewsbury line would provide a direct link with a projected marshalling yard at Walcot. Sadly, this plan did not materialise and the Silverdale Junction-Madeley Chord section was finally closed in August 1966 — all regular workings having ceased in the preceding February. The Wellington-Nantwich Junction line had not much longer to live and the end came on Monday 1 May 1967, almost 104 years after the triumphant opening of Market Drayton's first railway. In effect, the railway situation had reverted to those mid-Victorian days; henceforward freight for the Market Drayton district would have to be collected from either Whitchurch or Nantwich stations and while a British Rail spokesman was quoted as saying that he did not think the shut-down would affect local tradespeople to any great extent, others did not share his complacency and the *Newport & Market Drayton Advertiser* described the move as a 'backward march into progress'.

The eastern part of the former Knotty branch has fared rather better. Although the section between Stoke (Newcastle Junction) and Liverpool Road bridge at Newcastle was abandoned in 1967 — when Newcastle station site was brought up to the level of King Street and the two tunnels were packed with colliery waste — a single line from Apedale Junction to Madeley Chord has been retained as the only rail link with the thriving collieries at Silverdale and Holditch (alias Brymbo). The latter is served from the Apedale branch (as it has been since the pit was sunk in 1918) and at Silverdale an overhead hopper has been installed for the working of 'merry-go-round' coal trains to and from the power stations at Rugeley and Ironbridge. The Ironbridge traffic is routed via Stafford to Wolverhampton, where a reversal on to the erstwhile GWR line takes the trains through Shifnal to a further junction which, curiously enough, is also named 'Madeley', from the Shropshire village nearby. The signal box at Madeley Chord had a short life, being removed in 1971, since when overall control has been exercised from the main line box at Madeley, the three miles from Silverdale to Holditch being worked as one continuous siding, Apedale Junction box has also been dismantled and the reversals there are effected by ground levers. In 1960-1, the notorious 'slum landlord' Peter Rachman purchased over 400 acres of

Apedale land and for a time there were hopes that the area would once again become a hive of industry. Financial problems intervened, however, and by the time of Rachman's sudden death, in November 1962, the venture had collapsed.

This story therefore begins and ends with methods of extracting minerals from the Apedale valley. The 200-odd years between have witnessed many changes, but one may imagine that old Sir Nigel Gresley would have approved the sight of two Class '25' diesel locomotives rolling through Knutton Gate with up to a thousand tons behind them. In fact, this remnant of the Market Drayton branch seems set to last for many years to come; in October 1976 the National Coal Board announced plans for extensive future mining operations in the area, which are expected to yield 1,000,000 tons of coal annually until well into the twenty-first century and the Silverdale Colliery is particularly proud of its consistently high output.

Elsewhere, however, it is already difficult to find traces of railway occupation — especially at Market Drayton, where the station site is now an industrial estate and the long-awaited by-pass road overlays the one-time GWR tracks for some distance. At Pipe Gate the main Stone-Nantwich road (A51), which was diverted to an under-line bridge when the branch was constructed, has been restored to its original course and the station buildings have been demolished — as at Madeley Road. The buildings at Silverdale are intact and the single line token instrument is housed in the former booking office, Keele is derelict and Norton-in-Hales has been converted into a dwelling house, some of the matching material from Pipe Gate having been utilised for extensions. At the time of writing, the goods warehouses and yard at Newcastle are still identifiable as railway premises (a wagon turn-plate is discernible at the Brunswick Street end) but the whole area has been taken over as a depository for scrap metal. East of the tunnels the landscape has been changed dramatically by the construction of the Potteries 'D-road' (A500) which forms an arterial link between the motorway intersections at Hanchurch and Barthomley, a fitting comment on a revolution in transport.

Here and there embankments have been levelled, cuttings filled and the land returned to agricultural use. For a few more years, though, the railway will live on in personal memory, and during my research several people kindly offered their recollections of days past, to which I may add some of my own, in the hope that these will be of general interest. Unfortunately, although as a schoolboy I travelled from Pipe Gate to Market Drayton between 1927 and 1934, I gained little knowledge of the Great Western's services to the town — apart, that is, from occasional school outings (always to places on the GWR), summer holidays spent at Shrewsbury (change at Wellington) and one memorable trip to the Liverpool & Manchester centenary exhibition in

1930. Two of my schoolfellows were the sons of station masters at Hodnet and Tern Hill.

Memories of the Knotty branch are more numerous. Mr J S Funival, of Bearstone, who was among the first pupils at the re-constituted grammar school at Market Drayton (in 1910) informed me that as the railway ran through his father's farm land he was 'allowed' to walk along the line to Norton-in-Hales station to catch the train to school — and how the watchful platelayers' 'ganger' promised him one old penny for every tuft of 'squitch grass' he could find en route. In fact the permanent way was kept so meticulously that young Furnival was never able to claim a reward, and as evidence of the good husbandry of those days, it may be mentioned that the grass on either side of the tracks was carefully harvested and stacked at strategic points, from where it was removed by train to help feed the company's dray horses at Stoke.

Mr Morris, formerly of Silverdale, remembered stirring scenes in the station yard during World War I, when troops and supplies were frequently passing to and from the camps in Keele park; he also stressed that when he was a child 'practically everything' for the villagers' needs was brought in by rail — including the beer for the many public houses of this typical mining community. Incidentally, Mr Morris was able to confirm that stone from the Racecourse pit at Silverdale was conveyed by horse-drawn 'tumbrils' to a loading stage on what had undoubtedly been a part of Sneyd's railway, near Knutton forge. This pit took its name from a racecourse which had been laid out in 1778 and which reached the height of its popularity during the Regency period. The surrounding land was enclosed in 1818 but racing continued for a further thirty years under the auspices of the Newcastle corporation and the so-called 'Newcastle and Pottery' meetings attracted large crowds. Eventually the site was relinquished to mining purposes and Sneyd's Silverdale & Newcastle Railway Act of 1859 stipulated, inter alia, that facilities were to be given for the formation of 'collateral branch lines' if such were desired by the owners of land within 300yds of Sneyd's railway. These owners included the Lords of the Manor of Knutton, who were thereby granted leave to construct a siding 'from a point not exceeding two furlongs northwards (sic) from the junction of the North Staffordshire Railway.' However, although traces of a levelled way between the loading stage and the pit site were visible until recent years, there was no evidence that a standard gauge siding (or 'collateral branch') had ever been laid and Mr Morris' recollection is therefore of interest.

Mr Snape, who was the last joint station master at Pipe Gate and Norton-in-Hales, told me that a highlight of his long term of office was the overnight stop of Prime Minister Winston Churchill's special train in the cutting west of Pipe Gate station. The occasion was a visit to bomb-damaged Merseyside during World War II and it was said that souvenir hunting villagers afterwards searched the line for discarded cigar butts! On a more mundane note, a lady from Halmerend, who travelled by train from Keele to Market Drayton on Wednesdays during the mid-1930s, remembered that sometimes the serial number of her ticket followed on from the previous week . . . a clear indication of falling passenger receipts.

My boyhood memories are centred upon Pipe Gate station which, in the 1920s, was still well-kept with small rock gardens here and there and a fine show of geraniums surrounding the windows of the signal box. The booking office and waiting rooms were unusually placed at rail level, to the east of the up platform and there was a proper brick and tile waiting room (complete with NSR stove pot) on the opposite platform — unlike the open 'waiting shed' which served the other branch stations apart from Newcastle. I remember watching the dilatory shunting operations that took place each morning and after-noon (was it *always* summertime?) — the soft 'chink-chink' of *Snow-don's* cross-head pump as she sidled up to a line of milk vans beside the down platform — of privileged visits to the signal box, a sizeable affair with a 32-lever frame, and of pitting my strength against the up distant, a lofty double-armed signal a thousand yards away. Nor do I forget a Sunday morning in April 1932, when one of the pneumatic-tyred railcars ('Michelines') which had been developed in association with the Michelin Tyre Company, ran along the Knotty branch on its way to a trial on the S.R. at Ascot. The railcar was halted at Market Drayton for a short while before leaving for Wellington, during which time the townspeople were invited to inspect 'this revolutionary advancement in rail transport'.

On Saturday 25 April 1964 I took part in an enthusiasts' rail tour (organised by the Branch Line Society) which ventured on to the crumbling Apedale and Pool Dam branches as well as the line from Chatterley to Chesterton. 'Owing to the nature of the lines concerned' the special was confined to half a dozen brake vans, hauled by 2-6-0 locomotive No 78056, so that the tour's billing as 'the first and last public passenger train' to those areas was something of a misnomer. Nevertheless, this journey was particularly memorable to me in mark-ing the end of a long acquaintance with the Market Drayton branch — and surely one does not have to be a 'railwayac' to regret the passing of yet another country branch line!

ACKNOWLEDGMENTS

The author gratefully acknowledges the detailed help and encouragement he has received from Dr J R Hollick and Mr G N Nowell-Gossling, co-authors of the first history of the North Staffordshire Railway (1952). He also thanks Messrs H B Holland, N Rowley and E Talbot for their valued assistance as well as the staffs of the Horace Barks Reference Library at Hanley, the Local Studies Library at Shrewsbury and the William Salt Library at Stafford.

BIBLIOGRAPHY

The North Stafforshire Railway — 'Manifold'
The North Staffordshire Railway — Christiansen & Miller
The Shropshire & Montgomeryshire Railway — Tonks
Newport & Market Drayton Advertiser
Staffordshire Sentinel
Staffordshire Advertiser
Railway Magazine (various issues).

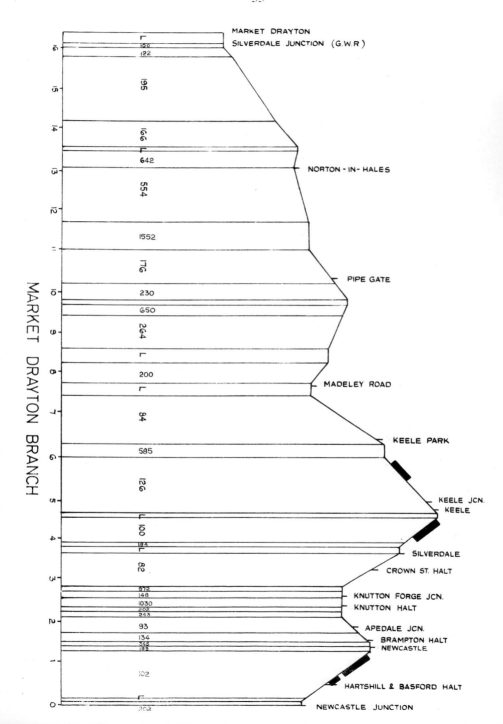

NORTH STAFFORDSHIRE RAILWAY.   KEELE VILLAGE.

NORTH STAFFORDSHIRE RAILWAY.   WINNINGTON WATERFALL, PIPE GATE STATION.

NORTH STAFFORDSHIRE RAILWAY.   PUBLIC FOOTPATH BLACKBROOK TO RADWOOD,
                                              MADELEY ROAD STATION.

In 1912 the North Staffordshire Railway issued a series of six postcards illustrating villages and countryside along the Stoke to Market Drayton line. Three of the set are shown here, the remainder can be found on the rear cover.

J. Alsop Collection